letters from new orleans
rob walker

GARRETT COUNTY PRESS

Garrett County Press First Edition 2005

For more information address:

GARRETT COUNTY PRESS

828 Royal St. #248

New Orleans, LA 70116

www.gcpress.com

PRINTED IN THE U.S.A.

GARRETT COUNTY PRESS BOOKS ARE PRINTED ON ACID FREE PAPER.

INTERIOR DESIGN BY KAREN OCKER

JACKET PHOTOGRAPH BY D.E. GOODFAB

Library of Congress Cataloging-in-Publication Data

Walker, Rob, 1968-
    Letters from New Orleans / by Rob Walker. — Garrett County Press 1st ed.
    p. cm.
    ISBN 1-891053-01-9 (alk. paper)
    1. Walker, Rob, 1968—Homes and haunts—Louisiana—New
Orleans—Anecdotes. 2. City and town life—Louisiana—New
Orleans—Anecdotes. 3. New Orleans (La.)—Social life and
customs—Anecdotes. 4. New Orleans (La.)—Description and
travel—Anecdotes. 5. New Orleans (La.)—Biography—Anecdotes. I. Title.
    F379.N55W35 2005
    976.3'35064'0922—dc22

                                    2004021597

letters from new orleans

dedicated to E

A BRIEF INTRODUCTION

Just before January 1, 2000, I moved from New York City to New Orleans, with my girlfriend, E. I began to write about our new home, eventually distributing *The Letter From New Orleans* — "pointless, sporadic, and free" — via email, to friends and, later, to strangers who were interested for one reason or another. All fourteen *Letters*, and some other dispatches concerning New Orleans, follow. They appear chronologically, but can, and maybe should, be read in some other order of your own devising. This is not a memoir, a history, or an exposé. It is just a modest series of stories about a place that means a lot to me. I never figured the *Letters* would end up in a book. But here they are.

ROB WALKER

to new orleans

day 1

Random bullets are a problem in New Orleans, especially on New Year's Eve. Apparently it's something of a tradition among certain locals to step outside and pop off a few rounds. I just moved here with E, my girlfriend, and we didn't know about this. Then she noticed a billboard showing a hand firing a gun into the air and the warning "Falling Bullets Kill." And I read in the paper that "police officials urge residents…to avoid firing weapons into the air." Somehow "avoid" seems a little nonchalant to me. I think one *avoids* fatty foods; one simply *does not fire* weapons into the air in an urban setting, even on special occasions.

But maybe that just goes to show that I have a lot to learn about my new home.

The Time Out Guide to New Orleans notes: "Orleanians are proud of their culture. ... Visitors are expected to be as enthusiastic about the city as the natives are. If you like the city, tell everyone; if you're not happy in New Orleans, keep it to yourself."

• • •

In addition to falling bullets, the reasons *not* to move to New Orleans include: a largely moribund economy (though it's perkier than it was), a high crime rate (though this, too, has improved), crushing summer heat, and the legitimate possibility of being wiped out by a hurricane or flood. These are good reasons. The population here has fallen from about 628,000 in 1960 to 466,000 in 1998.

So why are we here? We're here, actually, because we really are as enthusiastic about the city as the natives are. This is the second time I've moved across the country; the first was from Texas, which is where I'm from, to New York City, where I spent the last eight or so years. I had a good job as an editor (at a big-deal magazine), and E had a good job as a graphic designer (at a big-deal design firm). We liked New York and we have many wonderful friends there.

But to make a long story short, we just like it here more right now. We're in this great big duplex — or "half double," as the local parlance has it — instead of our awful little Greenwich Village railroad apartment. We live in a quiet, pretty neighborhood. It's been about 75 degrees and sunny every day so far. We like the food, the music, the way people talk. And, maybe more to the point, it's been such a short time that it still feels like we're on vacation. What we have is a big, huge crush on New Orleans. We're walking around thinking, "Oh, falling bullets, that's not such a bad thing, I'm sure it's just a phase."

• • •

When you move a long way, to a place you don't know very well, life is a weird mix of quotidian tasks and we're-new-to-these-parts wandering. Yesterday, Sunday, we hunted down a *New York Times*, stopped at Ace Hardware for some paint, and bought some coffee filters. Then we shifted to tourist mode and drove around to various points on the levee that keeps the Mississippi from flowing across New Orleans' streets, some of which, I gather, are as many as 18 feet below sea level. Eighteen feet! I just finished John Barry's excellent book about the 1927 Mississippi flood, *Rising Tide* — which a New Orleans acquaintance insisted I read before crossing her threshold again — and I wanted to look at the river.

I can't say I feel quite at home yet, although I came close on New Year's Eve. First we went down to the French Quarter, but it was choked with foolish young drunkards from the four corners of the New South, so we scurried back to our new neighborhood — Bayou St. John, or Faubourg St. John, or simply Over by the Whole Foods — and went to the local bar. Liuzza's by the Track, this place is called, and there were four people there at 11:20. We ordered drinks. E is a little obsessed with Liuzza's, because it seems like a real neighborhood place, it's very unpretentious, the gumbo is good, there is Abita on tap, the clientele is friendly and so is the bartender. At 11:35 or so people started showing up. Regulars. Everyone in the bar knew everyone else, I think, except us. Some brought their own bottles of champagne; some brought their own champagne glasses; one woman literally danced through the door with both. With maybe 20 people, the place felt full by 11:45. A guy bought a round for the house. Janis Joplin sang "Bobby McGee" on the jukebox. We all looked at the TVs for the big countdown. It was a wonderful moment.

The next morning I walked over to the Circle K and bought

the paper, which said that five people had been hit by random bullets, fallen from the sky.

day 2

Before we moved here, I figure I had spent a total of 20 days in New Orleans, over a period of 12 years; I guess E had spent about 15 days here over two years or so. So it's silly to claim we have "favorite" local spots, but there's a bar called Donna's where we've spent a couple of great evenings, and we are going again tonight. Donna's is known for traditional brass-band music, and one of the cool things is the number of young musicians we have seen there.

It's interesting to think about *traditional* music. We took a trip to Ireland over the summer, and one of the best experiences we had there was seeing a little "traditional" band play a set-dancing gig in a big barn in Kilfenora. I grew up in a small town in Texas (but not as small as Kilfenora). And it occurred to me that many of the people I basically looked down on there — the kickers (as we called them) who wore Wranglers and chewed tobacco and listened to KIKK, the big country music station out of Houston — those people were *traditional*. (Of course, many of them didn't think very highly of me, either, but that's another story.) The point is that I now have a little more respect for young people who cleave to the local traditions, whatever they might be. In a lot of ways, it's far easier to rebel against or reject the local thing and copy whatever they're doing on MTV.

On the other hand, the music on KIKK was *really* awful.

. . .

Anyway, the music at Donna's doesn't start until 10. So that leaves the day open for Tasks. As a result I spent a lot of time driving around. The good news is that I am enjoying driving, which I obviously didn't do much of while living in Manhattan. The bad news is I'm driving a rental and I'm essentially in denial about the fact that it's due back Friday and I have to buy a car. I  haven't owned one since 1992, when I sold mine to a used-car dealer in Dallas named Ronnie Diamond. For the past eight years the car experience for me has meant: You get to the airport in wherever, you go to the Avis counter, they give you the keys to some late-model sedan with about 800 miles on it, you zip around without ever wondering about whether it needs oil, and then you give it back.

I'm going to miss that.

So: Tasks. You don't want to hear about the tasks. We had to buy some stuff. It was a big hassle. There was traffic. E's comment: "You mean you're not going to write about us fighting about the furniture?"

• • •

Donna's is at the edge of the Quarter, right across Rampart from the gaudily lit entrance to Louis Armstrong Park. Five-dollar cover. The place has a lived-in feel. It's not a theme park; it's divey in a good way. Disconcertingly, there's carpet over much of the floor. Also, there is a parked motorcycle in here that I don't remember. The bathroom is behind the performance area, so you have to walk through the band to get there. Donna herself is behind the bar tonight. There's a good crowd, probably helped by the fact that the Sugar Bowl — you know, the *Nokia* Sugar Bowl — is tomorrow.

10:30 p.m.: The band starts — trumpet, trombone, piano, bass, guitar, drums. A mostly traditional set list; funny, gravelly voiced leader who knows how to work a crowd.

11:15 p.m.: At about this time of the night, I start thinking about traditional-ness again. Is it the sincerity that's attractive? That seems like such a cliché.

11:35 p.m.: Red beans, rice, and barbecued chicken are

made available, for free. I get a plate. Tasty.

12:45 a.m.: We're into the second set by now. Donna is dancing away behind the bar, doing that shimmy-bop stomp that works with New Orleans rhythm. I decide it's not sincerity, it's unselfconsciousness. That's what I like about Donna's, and about the way certain musicians play traditional, and about this city: I like the unselfconsciousness.

1:15 a.m.: A woman at the bar next to E gives her a tiny bag with a string attached, like a necklace. She puts this around E's neck and says: Close your eyes and make a wish, then look inside for your fortune. She does the same with me. I wish for an idea about how to end the diary I have to write when I get home. I open up the bag and there's a tiny painting, and some lines from Lao-Tzu, including: "Care about other people's approval and you will be their prisoner."

As we leave, the band is still playing.

day 3

We don't have any plans tonight. It's a little unsettling. Neither of us has family here, and only a couple of friends. At this point I would say we know six people in New Orleans, one of whom I've actually only met via phone.

Moving to a new city is not all fun and games, even if the new city is New Orleans. This morning we waited for the dishwasher repair guy to arrive. Then I spent a long time on the phone with BellSouth arranging for an additional phone line. After that there was shopping to be done at the Winn-Dixie. Hovering in the background: a hangover.

We are about 70 percent unpacked, I think. I've been saying this for days. That's because once you're 70 percent unpacked, you can stop. You've got all the useful stuff out, and you know where to find all the un-useful stuff — a big tangle of extra stereo wire; a 1986 paperback called *The Making of Miami Vice*, by Trish Janeshutz and Rob MacGregor; that sort of thing — if you happen to need it, which you never will. So on a day like today I really ought to just finish unpacking. I think I'll go for a walk.

I've been walking around our neighborhood a lot, just wandering back and forth to the grocery store or taking the dog out for a stroll. There's no logic to the architectural styles. But you notice two things. One is that the houses are built high, and often there's a big, massive, marvelous staircase of some sort leading up to a porch and a front door that might be three feet or even six feet off the ground. This, of course, is

because it can flood here in a really serious way. The second thing you notice is that the yards, the steps, the porches, the areas in front of the house are often just covered with plants in big pots, and statues, and chairs, and things. Just strewn all over, as if they were indoors and protected, as if nothing could ever threaten them, not man or nature. These yards and porches are often incredibly beautiful. And in their way, they seem to me a pretty convincing manifestation of pure denial.

• • •

Now it's about 6 in the evening and it's clear that I'm not really getting any unpacking done. We're leafing through the paper instead. Says here two men arrested for firing weapons into the air on New Year's Eve are now out on bond. Meanwhile, one of the five people hit by falling bullets that night remains in Charity Hospital.

I haven't said anything about food, and of course everyone knows that New Orleans is a great food town. I don't really have anything new to say on the subject of excellent local food, but I *can* offer this: The other night, one of our half-dozen New Orleans acquaintances discoursed for us on some local bake shop or other that's well known for poundcake and advertises that it ain't called *poundcake* for nothing 'cos there's a *pound* of butter in there, and further advertises that it might be good to Try It Fried!

There you go. Fried poundcake.

• • •

The actor Philip Michael Thomas played Ricardo Tubbs, sidekick of Don Johnson's character, Sonny Crockett, on the popular television drama *Miami Vice*. The show was so popular that Thomas managed to convince someone to let him record an album. But that album, Trish Janeshutz and Rob MacGregor reported in 1986, "is just one facet of Thomas's five-year plan, EGOT. That stands for Emmy, Grammy, Oscar and Tony, the awards he has set out to win for his performances in TV, on record, on film, and on stage. He wears a gold medallion emblazoned with the letters as a reminder of his goals."

Can you imagine? Do you think that's true — he wore a medallion that said EGOT? Does he still have it? I don't think he won any of those awards; in fact I'd be surprised if he was even nominated for any.

I should return this book to the guy who loaned it to me. I think this is the third time I've moved it.

Well, anyway, it sure is getting late. E and I have made some plans after all. We're going out to eat, then heading over to a bar uptown to see some jazz.

Tomorrow will be more productive.

Today's theme has been: denial.

day 4

I forgot to mention the stolen car. E drove down here before me with our dog, Rey, and on her first or second night in New Orleans, her rental car was stolen from the street right in front of the house. We actually have a gated driveway, but the landlord hadn't yet given E the combination to the lock on it. We'd both heard quite a bit about New Orleans' storied problems with crime, but this happened so quickly that it kind of stunned us; grand theft auto focuses the mind wonderfully.

E told this story to a car salesman today. (I test drove four cars, ranging from a new VW Beetle to a Jeep Cherokee; I obviously have no idea what I'm doing.) The car salesman had just told us how, shortly before Christmas, two guys had somehow broken into this dealership in the middle of the night and driven a car off the showroom floor, through a plate-glass window. Just smashed right on through. Ha ha! Everybody here has a crime story. Sometimes the teller just seems intent on scaring the hell out of you. Other times the teller simply wraps it up with a laugh.

In this case the two guys who ripped off the dealership were caught a few hours later; apparently they'd smashed both mirrors off the vehicle, so they were somewhat easily spotted. I guess that's funny.

The Times-Picayune editorial page came out strongly against "celebratory gunfire" today. There's been some confusion as to

how stiff a penalty can be laid on someone convicted of illegal discharge of a weapon: The mayor had threatened up to seven years in prison, but the DA has since pointed out that the actual maximum is two years. The paper argued that city leaders need to get this stuff straight and work together against the problem. "There's no excuse for negligent gunowners to go out and randomly fire their weapons into the sky."

Sorry to keep coming back to this topic, but the random bullet problem really seems like something out of a Don DeLillo novel to me. And maybe it says something about the character of New Orleans; I'm not sure. Is it worth trying to pin down the character of a city in a few sentences? It's a dicey business, especially with a city like New Orleans that's been written about so often. Listen to an attempt to capture the French

Quarter: "Outside the window New Orleans, the vieux carré, brooded in a faintly tarnished languor like an aging yet still beautiful courtesan in a smokefilled room, avid yet weary too of ardent ways." Feh! You know who that is? That's *William Faulkner*, from a novel called *Mosquitos*. If that's what Faulkner comes up with, maybe I shouldn't try.

• • •

So, back to idiotic criminal acts: Someone made the case a couple of months ago that a brisk economy siphons off a certain percentage of the criminal class who are smart enough to see that in times like these it's easier to make money legitimately than by, say, driving cars through plate-glass windows. As these people pass into the regular economy, only the dopiest and least competent criminals are left behind, and thus crime falls.

I don't know whether that's true or not. But here's how the story of E's rental car getting stolen turned out. About a day after the car disappeared — after she had called the cops, and the rental-car people, and her credit-card company — she was walking to a nearby convenience store. And she spotted the stolen rental car, being pushed into the convenience store's parking lot by three kids. Apparently they had stolen the car and driven it around the neighborhood, until they *ran out of gas.*

Obviously, she didn't confront them herself but hailed a cop, and the long and the short of it is that the kids got away but the rental company got its car back, and we have since learned the combination to the lock on our little gated driveway. The point is that E has told this story a bunch of times, and so have I, and when the car salesman heard it, he laughed, and we laughed right along with him. Ha ha!

day 5

Ahem. Now that we're at the end of this diary, I thought I would answer the most Frequently Asked Questions about the move that E and I made, from New York City to New Orleans.

Q: Why did you choose New Orleans?

A: In Manhattan, I found, one tends to think in terms of What's New. For example, I can remember when Balthazar was the new Bowery Bar, when Moomba was the new Spy Bar, and when Orchard Street became the new Ludlow Street and Thursday was the new Friday. Right before I left, I realized that Smith Street (in Brooklyn!) had become the new Elizabeth Street. Last year people said gray was the new black. For a minute or two, sincerity was supposed to be the new irony. I saw on a magazine cover that brown was the new blond. About two years ago someone told me that Beat poetry was the new broccoli rabe. Certainly I remember Avenue B becoming the new Avenue A, and I think by now Avenue C is the new Avenue B. The idea is to have spotted the It Idea five minutes before whoever you're talking to. I'm not really criticizing this game. It was sort of fun. So...What's New? Is Dave Eggers the new Kurt Andersen? Is Pastis the new Balthazar and the meatpacking district the new SoHo? Well: Maybe New Orleans is the new Avenue C!

Q: Why did you choose New Orleans?

A: There's a place, about five minutes from our house by way of Carrollton Avenue, called Rock n' Bowl. That's where we went last night. Wednesday and Thursday nights are zydeco nights, and there is usually a first-rate zydeco band (we once saw Beau Jacques here on a 1998 visit) and a crowd that's black and white, and young and old. We made a trip out to the dance floor, but mostly we watch, because everyone else seems to dance so well. Also, if you don't want to dance at all, there is bowling. Eighteen lanes. Who wouldn't want to live in a city that has Rock 'n' Bowl? We stayed for only one set this time, but it ended well after midnight.

Q: Why did you choose New Orleans?

A: Once "Page Six" was available online, it became possible to live anywhere. There's no reason that the new Avenue C might not be beyond the East Village, beyond Williamsburg or Long Island City. It could be anywhere. *Right*?

Q: Why did you choose New Orleans?

A: Some cities really do have personalities, good or bad. One of the themes in the background of the very fine David Shields book *Black Planet*, about a season spent obsessing over the Seattle Supersonics, is the insecurity that is apparently fundamental to the character of Seattle. That's a city personality that I would dislike. I lived in Dallas, and the place seemed to tremble with insecurity, always wondering what the coasts think. Houston, on the other hand, is authentically uninterested in the opinions of outsiders. Austin is smug, still convinced that it's Paris in the '20s. New York is New York. Boston isn't. Denver has no personality. Neither does Orlando. San Francisco is all about convincing anyone who listens that it is *the future* — it's the new New York! Miami is a bit like that, too. And in a way so is Atlanta. Anyway, I like a city that doesn't waste time trying to convince anyone of anything — I like a city that's chauvinistic.

Q: Why did you choose New Orleans?

A: New Orleans is not the new Avenue C. This was once the richest city in the South. It is not that anymore, but it is also not the *new* anything; it is *still* New Orleans. What does that mean? I think random bullets are a clue. I think unselfconsciousness is a clue. Denial is a clue. Laughing at trouble seems like a clue, and so does dancing at Rock n' Bowl. Of course, I'll look back on all this in a a year or two, or more, and be amazed at how badly I read the clues, at how little I understood, early on, about the mysteries of this place. It will all seem clearer then, I hope. Because that's why we chose New Orleans.

JANUARY 3-7, 2000

3% theory

In the summer of 1988, when I was a student in Austin, Texas, I interviewed a guy named Kal Spelletich for an article I was writing for the college paper about performance art. The article was forgettable and sophomoric (I was a sophomore), but some of the conversations I had while reporting it, particularly my conversations with Spelletich, stayed with me. He was a grad student at the time, and a founder of a performance group called Seemen.

Partly for the story, I went to a couple of events at a place called Austin Media Arts, which was basically a large, windowless room above a café on Guadalupe. Performance art gets a lot of abuse, and maybe a lot is deserved, but I saw some cool stuff there. In any case Spelletich was the person who introduced me to the word "ephemeral." And something else: He was from Iowa, and I think I asked something along the lines of, Isn't it a relief to be somewhere cooler than Iowa, where you can find like-minded people? "There's always a fringe element," he answered. "You could go to Waco, Texas, and 3 percent of the people are going to be these experimental artists." Obviously that's not true in a literal sense, but I take 3 percent to mean "a small number" and experimental artists to mean "interesting and unconventional people" or maybe "weirdos." Since that conversation, I've thought of this as the Three Percent Theory.

Later I moved to Dallas, and then to New York, where I spent most of the 1990s and where I met E. Seven or eight months ago we moved to New Orleans. We've met a lot of great people, but I don't have anything like the "social obligations" I had in New York, and by that I mean that on Friday afternoon we had no plans for the weekend at all and I was flipping through the local paper's entertainment section. There was a listing for "Seemen Interactive Performance...the San Francisco-based project features interactive robots ..."

• • •

The Zeitgeist Multi-Disciplinary Arts Center is on Oretha Castle Haley Boulevard. Just a few blocks from the fancy homes on the celebrated St. Charles Avenue, it's an outpost in one of these sections of town that seems to be all abandoned buildings — beautiful in their way, but apparently on the verge of collapse. Zeitgeist is a classic Three Percent establishment, a generous space, built a long time ago for some other forgotten purpose, with concrete floors, a lot of local art on the walls, and "Heroin," by the Velvet Underground, playing in the background. There was an incongruous Ryder truck nearby; it was full of robots.

The newspaper listed the start time as 9:30, but of course it was about 11:15 when Spelletich began his spiel. He looked almost exactly as he had 12 years earlier, like a nice, clean Midwesterner with short hair, a big smile, T-shirt and shorts. He talked quickly and almost goofily, like a kid in front of his first audience ever. Apparently he'd come to New Orleans in connection with a computer graphics convention, and had managed to hook up with Zeitgeist and schedule this appearance at the last second. He mentioned that he had now taken his robots to 40 cities in the United States and Europe, and always managed to find a space and a crowd. Cleveland. Detroit. Everywhere.

He turned his attention to the first contraption, a skeletal metal torso in a simple dress, her "legs" ending in a wide, round base, and with a kind of elaborate nozzle for a head. An audience member was given the controls to make the "Whirling Dervish" spin frantically. Spelletich said: "But something's missing, right?" An adjustment was made, and now the audience member made the Dervish whirl again, but this time spewing several feet of flame from the place where her head should be.

• • •

Spelletich had a scene in *Slacker*, in which he wore a TV backpack that was part of the Seemen repertoire then, and talked about the disappointment of seeing a real-life stabbing that failed to match the verisimilitude of the many violent deaths he'd seen on television and in the movies. Years later, in New York, I somehow heard that the Seemen name was still around, Spelletich was living in San Francisco, he'd had some involvement with Survival Research Laboratories, and was doing work involving pyrotechnic robots. Apparently these had even appeared at Burning Man, and I knew that he/they had performed at least once in New York, but for whatever reason I missed it.

So it was a pleasure to be in that parking lot, with all this metal and all these butane tanks strewn across the ground along with a couple of theatrical "Danger" signs and a crowd sipping beer and volunteering. "I have no insurance," Spelletich announced, with his big, innocent smile. "No joke." All the robots involved fire. A woman who claimed to work at an investment bank strapped on an elaborate belt that shot fire from the crotch. ("So now you get it," Spelletich said to her. "The guy thing.") Another woman climbed into a cage and held on as another big sheet of fire swatted against the bars. The most dazzling and popular attraction involved standing in the center of a giant cylinder and presumably trying to remain as still as possible while four bars are set alight and sent spinning, leaving the volunteer enveloped in fire. The people who tried that looked a little shaken afterwards.

What's good about all this? Playing with fire — a bit immature, no? Maybe so. What's good about it to me is that it all seems so improbable. Fire-belching, homemade robots in some cracked parking lot — it sounds vaguely illegal. Everything that's good about it really is ephemeral, from the overall incongruity of the scene to the unspecified danger to the feeling of the heat on your face. The audience can never get big, there's no money it, he'll never be on Letterman. I guess it's impossible to capture the thing in so many non-ephemeral words after the moment has passed, and that's the point. That, and the further confirmation of the Three Percent Theory.

The last bit of fire drifted into the sky at about midnight. Spelletich, rather warmly, thanked us all for coming.

AUGUST 2000

carnival

On a recent Friday night, E and I finished touching up our skeleton costumes. They aren't very complicated: Black sweatpants and shirts overlaid with stencils depicting the outlines of bones, which we filled in with special white paint. Add storebought rubber masks. This was the outfit worn by all thirty or forty members of our sub-krewe — the Krewe du Lewd — and it was in these outfits that we walked the long parade route from Faubourg Marigny, through the French Quarter, throwing beads.

Last year we had a very nice Mardi Gras, our first. In part I think this was because we had no expectations, or maybe negative ones. Now, I am no expert on Mardi Gras, or Carnival, but I have learned a few things — such as the difference between Mardi Gras and Carnival. The latter, as you may know, refers to a season, beginning on the Feast of the Epiphany or King's Day or the Twelfth Night (January 6, twelve days after Christmas) and ending on Fat Tuesday (Mardi Gras), the day before Ash Wednesday.

I would say there are four interlocking versions of Mardi Gras here in New Orleans. There's the whole Bourbon Street thing. There's an extremely strange society ball circuit revolving around Carnival. There are parties. And there are the parades. The parades begin in earnest about ten days before Mardi Gras, and there are dozens of them in and around the city. We saw at least ten last year. Here is what happens: There are high school marching bands, and there are floats tugged by tractors. Each parade is put on by a krewe, which is what Carnival clubs are called. There is a theme for each parade, and the krewe members on the floats generally wear masks. What they do is they throw beads and other trinkets off the floats, and what you do, as a spectator, is try to get them to throw beads to you. You could, for example, jump up and down and yell. Or you could wear an elaborate wig. Et cetera.

(An example of a noun being verbed: Wearing a mask as a krewe member is referred to as "masking." "To mask." In an example of a verb being nouned, the beads and other items are hurled by the maskers are referred to as "throws." And so: "Because Jim will mask this year, he must buy some throws.")

So who are the krewe members? Well, it depends, and the details would take up too many words for such an informal note as this. Let's just say that some krewes are exclusive, and riding in some parades can be expensive, and leave it at that for now. It's time to get to this Mardi Gras, and the parade we joined, because that's what I want to tell about: being in a parade. So cut to:

Faubourg Marigny, the next neighborhood down river from the French Quarter. It actually looks like the Quarter, but a bit shabbier, and with smaller buildings and not as much for tourists to do. At the corner of Marigny and Chartres ("charters," in the proper New Orleans mispronunciation), somewhere between 800 and 1,000 Krewe du Vieux marchers loitered in a field, wearing a variety of costumes, many (but not all) of which were plainly obscene. The Krewe du Vieux styles itself a satirical comment on what is locally referred to as the "pageant" of Carnival, and for this reason there are usually a lot phalluses involved in this parade. Anyway, despite the claim to satire, what Krewe du Vieux really is, as is so often the case in New Orleans, is an excuse to behave foolishly in public.

We were invited to join in this year by a friend I'll call Dante. Actually, that's his name. The sub-krewe that Dante is part of — Krewe du Lewd — wears the skeleton outfits described

above, regardless of what the parade's theme is. This year's theme had something to do with outer space. We wore skeleton costumes.

In addition to people in costumes, the parade features a bunch of local brass bands, and a variety of "floats," which under the rules of the parade permit are small, jerry-rigged things that are pulled along by people, or by mules, not by the tractors that haul the big floats in the "real" parades. Many floats featured phalluses. Ours featured a big skull.

Many of the people in that field were drunk; certainly most of our sub-krewe was, since there had been a pre-parade party starting at about three in the afternoon, at which there was a large bowl of something that was supposed to be Long Island Iced Tea. It was more like Staten Island Iced Tea, but I had some anyway. Other krewe members had special cup holders that fit around their necks, so they could keep their hands free for bead throwing but still tote along fresh alcohol. It is of course perfectly legal to walk around New Orleans drinking alcohol freely, at any time.

It was dark, obviously, when the parade got underway, and I put on my rubber skeleton mask. It was good to wear a mask.

I hadn't done so since I was, I don't know, maybe seven years old, having scorned costume parties as an adult. It was a little sweaty and my visibility was not so good, but on the other hand the combination of being at the center of attention and totally anonymous, and hence not responsible for whatever might unfold, was intoxicating. No, it wasn't the liquor, it was the mask.

• • •

The first part of the parade route winds through the Marigny, and there most of the parade watchers are locals, meaning the crowds are modest in size and mellow in temperament. Still, they want beads. At first I hadn't thought the whole bead thing would be that interesting. But it's impossible — when the beads start flying off the floats, and everyone one around you is hollering for and catching them — it's impossible not to want to catch some beads yourself. You get swept up in it. And you holler and you rake in beads, and you lean over to catch strands that would have tumbled into the hands of a child and you pretend not to realize what you've just done. You start to get snooty about picking up beads off the ground (forget it!) and you become a connoisseur of beads, good ones and bad ones, rare ones and common ones. You know the difference. And so it is that the satisfaction from hurling that first set of beads

letters from new orleans

39

yourself, seeing it arc through the air and a bunch of hands straining up to catch it, and seeing one of those hands snap closed around the beads in mid-air, knowing that some modest little piece of delight has just been created where before there was only a strand of beads whose actual cash value is incalculably small — well, I tell you, that's the shit.

Here I'll just pause to mention that we bought our throws at Bead World on Tulane Avenue, which is not the best place, but it's where we went, a small shop just past all the bail bonds places. Your basic beads cost about 80 cents a dozen, which is actually sort of a ripoff, but whatever. We bought about $40 worth, and added to the massive pile of throws we caught last year and had decided to reintroduce to the Carnival Bead Ecosystem, this was all we could carry. Coincidentally, there was a story in the paper a few days later about Simon Zhent, who hails from the Chinese port city of Beihai, and who now owns Bead World. The Zhent family has a bead factory in China. That's where our beads ultimately came from. A knowledgeable bead man quoted in the story observed that most if not all Mardi Gras beads come from China, because "you have almost no labor costs there." The story did not dwell on the implications of this statement, and neither did I.

The parade lasts a long time, a couple of hours. It can be exhausting. We were right in front of one of the brass bands, which helped keep the energy up. Under normal circumstances,

I would find it impossible to dance along a street in public, but we were masked. So it was pretty easy. The mental challenge of figuring who to hand or throw beads to, trying to spot the person most likely to respond with a joyful yawp, or even a bashful smile, also helps. Plus the booze.

. . .

As we left the Marigny and crossed over into the Quarter, the crowds got bigger. We spotted someone we knew and E showered her with beads. The crowds got thicker. As you work your way toward Canal Street, you hit the part of the Quarter that is usually best to avoid, especially in the weeks before Mardi Gras. It was packed. There wasn't much in the way of crowd control, and the streets are narrow, and toward the end there was so much crowd that we were basically walking, or dancing, single file, through a sea of reaching hands. Tourists. They were starting to get belligerent. COME ON MAN GIVE ME SOME BEADS. BEADS! BEADS! COME ON! BEADS! I NEED BEADS!! Someone seemed to be waving money at me at one point. They were shouting at us. They were actually reaching and trying to take them out of our hands, off our necks. "You're missing the point," I said loudly to one guy, in a tone made possible by the skeleton mask.

Finally E and I were almost out of beads. We waltzed for a time. We were applauded for this, I assume because even the most obnoxious bead-craving parade-watcher likes to see two skeletons waltzing. The music, happily, had not deserted us even in the parade's most claustrophobic moments.

Although this finale was a little harrowing, on the whole I would say that if you ever have a chance to march in Krewe du Vieux, you should do it.

Finally the crowds tapered off as we got past Bourbon Street and more or less into the clear. The groups of onlookers were smaller and mannered again, and we entered the home stretch leading to the State Palace Theater, where there was a big Krewe Du Vieux party, and, of course, free beer. Outside the Palace we peeled of our masks. We figured that after this experience, it would be impossible ever to raise our hands and call out for beads again. But we were wrong about that.

MARCH 2001

the singing, the song

One morning not long ago I placed a phone call to the St. Paul
Spiritual Church of God in Christ, located in the Lower Ninth
Ward, just down river from the industrial canal in New
Orleans. Feeling slightly foolish, I explained to the nice woman
who answered that I had seen the church's choir perform at the
New Orleans Jazz & Heritage Festival and I wondered if, well, if
it would be okay, I guess, if anyone would mind if — if visitors
might be welcomed at a service. The nice woman said of course.
The service begins, promptly, at 11 a.m. on Sunday.

And so on a Sunday morning a week and half later E

and I and our friend Marc put on Sunday clothes and we went to church.

• • •

Jazz Fest takes place over two long weekends, on the grounds of a big horse-racing track about a 10-minute walk from our house. It's a large, sweaty, unwieldy event, with many acts performing simultaneously on many stages, all day long. These stages, and the food vendors, and the sellers of "crafts," take up the entire grassy area defined by the track itself. There's more over in the air-conditioned grandstand. Also, there are a couple of huge tents, or really small buildings made of canvass, standing on what is normally part of the parking lot.

One of these is the Gospel Tent. It's often said by devoted attendees that the very best place to spend a day at Jazz Fest is in the Gospel Tent. And so, on the festival's second Friday, I got to the tent at around 2 in the afternoon, as the Desire Community Choir was performing. The truth is that I chose this day because, according to the schedule, Michelle Shocked was supposed to sing with the St. Paul Spiritual Church of God in Christ choir. This appearance had attracted almost no advance attention, perhaps because interest in Michelle Shocked is limited.

The further truth is that I did not particularly enjoy the Desire Community Choir. I was distracted by the crowd, or the "scene." There were a lot of shirtless white guys drinking beer, for instance. They seemed to be enthusiastic about the music, and I'm not religious so I can hardly critique their engagement with the spiritual message. I just wasn't having a very good time.

• • •

On the day we went to church, we arrived at about 10:45 a.m. at an unassuming brick building. Of the 70 or so people in attendance we were the only three whites, which was not unexpected. The Lower Ninth Ward is one of many low-income, predominantly black neighborhoods in what is, after all, a low-income and predominantly black city. People looked at us, which was also not unexpected. I remember one young guy in an untucked white shirt giving me what I was pretty sure was a resentful glare.

But almost immediately people began to come over and greet us. Some sort of deputy pastor introduced himself. Everyone was warm. They shook our hands. Some asked where we currently "fellowship," and we dissembled. We did not, exactly, explain ourselves to anyone. Shortly before the service began, the kid I thought was glaring came over with a big loopy grin on and his face and shook hands with all of us.

• • •

Michelle Shocked did in fact perform with the choir at Jazz Fest. She wore tight black jeans and T-shirt, with a sliver of midriff exposed. She carried a white guitar. Her hair is now shoulder-length, brown, and I never would have recognized her. She explained that she *would* say she was honored by our applause, but that would be wrong. As wrong as saying that she and the choir were here merely to *entertain* us, because it's not about her, and it's not about the choir, and it's not about entertainment. It's about Jesus — and she's not ashamed to say that name! She went on like this for a while.

My heart sank. I have respect for the faithful. But I dislike holy-rollers who are so theatrical and pushy. I grew up around people who said things like this, who put Jesus in your face all the time, and basically I consider it rude. I pondered leaving.

Meanwhile, the St. Paul Spiritual Church of God in Christ choir filed on stage. There must have been 30 singers, forming two rows, mostly black, mostly young. Maybe there were two or three whites in choir. Michelle Shocked began to sing, and the choir began to sway. I don't really know my gospel numbers so well, and I'm terrible at picking out lyrics, but the song concerned "the rock." It built momentum. The other singers joined in on the chorus in an astonishing wave of sound. It was incredible, and I was swept up in it, filled with emotion. I was more or less choked up, okay?

I looked around. There was a thin white woman in a big straw hat, shorts, and high heels, balancing a plastic cup of beer and a camera. I didn't care. This sound, I decided, is the best thing I have heard at Jazz Fest this year. So I convinced E, and Marc, to come to church with me.

• • •

I guess I had imagined a stifling old room with wood floors and a vaulted ceiling and garish image of Christ on the cross, like something out of *The Apostle*. In fact the interior was carpeted, and air-conditioned, with modest but upholstered chairs, and, curiously, not a single religious symbol in sight.

There was a drum kit and two sets of keyboards. The music began. Five or six women were at the front, behind microphones. A couple of guys took turns leading a combination of music and preaching. For half an hour or so most everyone was on his or her feet, and, with the exception of us, singing and clapping along. There was a sense of dislocation that came with this — the music was coming from everywhere. It was transcendent, in the sense that being *within* the music seemed to lift, or maybe push, us *out* of the normal way our five senses perceive the world.

At various points we were all instructed to greet or even embrace our neighbors. Later there was a moment when people were positively flooding over to greet us, including many people who had already done so, but who moved from handshakes to hugs. Eventually the music stopped and the pastor began to speak. He spoke for a very long time; the sermon related to money. (I had no small bills on me, so in another non-surprise

I threw an absurd $20 into the collection jar.) As the morning and early afternoon wore on, late-arrivers kept coming, and I believe at the peak there must have been 120 or more people there, including three more whites, older than us.

Then, apropos of nothing, there came a point late in the service when the pastor announced to the room that there were some people here today who had come because they had heard the choir sing at Jazz Fest, and would these folks please stand up so everyone could recognize them for this compliment they were paying with their attendance?

We stood up to accept a round of applause. It was mortifying.

• • •

There's this line in an Eric Bogosian play in which a yuppie character looks back on his life and wipes away the notion that there might have been any hint of hypocrisy buried in his privileged lifestyle. Vis a vis those less fortunate, he says: "Hey, I was *concerned.*" Something about the Gospel Tent had made me feel as though I was in a place *zoned* for cultural curiosity, where people like me could take a seat and say to themselves: "Hey, I'm *open-minded.*" Take the shallowness of that sentiment and multiply by ten and you have a reasonable idea of how foolish I felt being applauded for barging into a place of worship to listen to music.

On the way out, again, everyone was wildly cheerful and

friendly to us. We shook hands with the pastor (who asked, hilariously, if we ourselves could sing) and told him, honestly, what a fine service it had been. And thinking about it later, I now believe I was misguided to be so embarrassed. Michelle Shocked had said that her relationship with this choir began on a day when she came to this very church just for the sake of the music. "I came for the singing," she declared, "but I stayed for the song." Now, I can't say that I heard "the song" in the way that she did, or that these various friendly parishioners do. But I finally realize that the song is what it's about at the St. Paul Spiritual Church of God in Christ, whether there are curious interlopers on hand to hear the morning's singing or not.

As we left, everyone said they hoped we would return. I can only assume that they meant it.

JUNE 2001

death and after

The first time I contemplated the face of a dead man, it was not a relative's or a close friend's. Instead, the deceased was Ernie K-Doe. The specifics of Ernie K-Doe will have to wait.⊙ For now, suffice it to say that he was an R&B singer and a New Orleans celebrity, or a semi-celebrity, partly on the strength of his 1961 hit "Mother In Law," but mostly on the strength of his outrageous personality and peculiar persona. And his large and flowing hair (or rather, I think, his wig). I often described K-Doe to visitors as a New Orleans version of Little Richard. His passing occasioned a jazz funeral this summer.

The jazz funeral is one of those practices that is closely associated with New Orleans – the sort of thing that invariably

⊙ SEE THE STORY "K-DOE."

pops up in novels or movies about the place. When I moved here I wondered: Do they really happen? What are they like? And because New Orleans is full of ersatz versions of famously New Orleans-y practices, I also wondered: Even if they really happen, are they really *real*? Here are three answers.

one

In November 2000, when I'd lived here for a little less than a year, I saw a listing in the local alternative weekly: "Jazz funeral, thus and so funeral home, 1716 N. Claiborne." They list funerals in the paper here? Is it cool to show up if you don't know the deceased? It must be if it's listed in the paper, right?

The funeral was scheduled to start at 3, and by then I'd learned that in New Orleans you should never be early for anything, because everything is late, always. I arrived by bike. The first person I noticed was an older black man wearing a electric-blue suit and sunglasses. Various others hung around, some white, some black. In this neighborhood white people tend to stand out. We looked like tourists. Anyway here I was, crashing a funeral, but it was in the paper and there were almost certainly some real tourists on hand, and actually two television cameras as well. Plus there were a couple of guys selling drinks and chips and so on, one out of his car trunk, another out of the back of an old Ford pickup. The latter guy walked by me and said, "Hey man we got cold drinks." I nodded. He said, "And beer."

I bought a can of Bud for two dollars. Beautiful day. People were showing up in cabs. Then someone walked by me with a bass drum: the band. I ventured a "How ya doin" to the tuba player and he said "All right," without looking at me. A horse-drawn carriage arrived. Two white horses, black man in a tuxedo at the reins. Old-fashioned casket on the back. I finished my beer.

Everybody was up now, moving into position, forming the "second line." The band struck some notes and the guy with the blue suit took his place in the lead. People started walking to the carriage and I pulled out my little point-and-shoot camera, but suddenly I was boxed out — everyone there had a camera or a video recorder. A documentation pile-on ensued as the entire crowd, for a few moments, consumed the moment. We were all there, and it really happened, and we could all prove it, I guess.

The parade — seventy people? — started moving. Some random guy, carrying a large window in one hand asked me: "Who died?" I admitted that I did not know who died. Now I really felt like an idiot. Window-guy nodded and kept walking, so I stopped to ask the potato chip vendor: "Who died?" He was an old, round man with few teeth and an incredibly wrinkled face, like a contour drawing, and he said, "Nobody! Ain't no body in there!" (He meant in the casket.) He explained that this was an event put on for the benefit of people who have never seen an actual jazz funeral. ("Tourists," he added, by way of example.)

Ah. I mentioned for no good reason that I live a short bike ride away. Then, disingenuously, I asked how everyone found out about it. "They been advertising it!" He showed me a flier pulled from his trunk.

two

A few months later, I was at home with E on a Monday afternoon. It was Martin Luther King Jr. day, but bleak outside, raining since the morning. We could hear some brass down on the street, trumpet and trombone. This isn't all that unusual where we live, but this time it didn't sound like Mardi Gras-related marching practice. From my window I could just see the movement of a small parade turning toward Broad from Gayoso, on St. Phillip.

We quickly put on jackets and darted around the corner. There was a small, five- or six-piece band and thirty or so others in front of a house, where another twenty people were gathered, dry, on the porch. All were black. The song was an upbeat number, but I didn't recognize it. Most of those on the rainy street were women, and they were dancing, some under umbrellas. They were drinking from green bottles of Heineken, and one woman was smoking a joint. She was in her stocking feet. Another woman was in stockings, too, and a black dress, and these two would lift up their skirts to dance. A white woman came out of the house next door with her baby and mingled with the crowd a bit, then went back inside and got a camera. The music segued into the slower "Just a Closer Walk with Thee." One of the shoeless women led others in some singing. Another tune started up and we decided to move along.

I assumed this was all somehow related to the holiday. Then a man in a baseball hat, missing some teeth, about 20 feet from the action, said something to us. Because of the noise from the band we had to ask him to repeat it.

"That's one tradition we will never give up," he said again.

It was a funeral. The man in the baseball hat explained that a woman in that house had cancer "real bad," and she had finally passed. "They buried her today, Martin Luther King Day," he said. "It's beautiful."

three

The evening before the Ernie K-Doe funeral, there was a wake at Gallier Hall. This is a Greek revival building downtown on St. Charles that was once the seat of city government, and is where the poobahs of New Orleans society now greet the Mardi Gras parades; in the past, various Confederate heroes lay in state there.

K-Doe was dressed in an elaborate white suit with sequined trim, white gloves, and a huge rhinestone tiara that served as a crown. A gold wand angled across his body, resting in his right hand. The casket was massive and ornate; K-Doe called himself The Emperor of The Universe. According to the program, his other nicknames included "Mr. Naugahyde" and "The Rhinestone Dresser." He was 65. In a bright room, under a painting of K-Doe that had been brought over from his club, the Mother In Law Lounge, we viewed the body. We had seen him perform several times. Now his face seemed to have settled in on itself; he did not look real.

Scores of people were there. We found our way into the room where the actual tribute service would occur and took seats off to one side. Soon it was full. So was another room where the proceedings were being echoed onto a TV screen. So was the broad hallway. The coffin containing the body of Ernie K-Doe was soon placed at the front of the room, beneath a microphone, where Allen Toussaint, Irma Thomas, and the mayor, among others, took turns speaking or singing. It happened that by sitting where we did, we were looking directly onto K-Doe's body for the entire service.

Eventually the band kicked into a full-on rendition of

"Mother In Law," and people were on their feet and dancing, dancing just feet from the open casket. We passed by K-Doe's body again on the way out, paid our respects, stared into his face. The paper said 5,000 people stopped by over the course of the day.

The next afternoon, hundreds and hundreds gathered outside Gallier Hall. It was hot. Umbrellas and parasols twirled in the crowd. A woman rode her pink bike, wearing a pink wig. There were a lot of wigs, there were shorts and there were suits. The crowd was black and white, locals and visitors, all ages. A horse-drawn carriage, possibly the same one I'd seen last October, waited in the street. Several brass bands lingered. The crowd grew.

Finally the doors to Gallier Hall opened, and the pall-bearers emerged with the coffin and other inner-circle mourners, all in sharp formalwear, tuxedos, top hats. Parting the crowd on the steep steps, they looked like royalty, and there was something about the scene that suggested historic importance and worldwide interest.

The carriage finally began to move down St. Charles toward Poydras Street, and we all fell in line behind it. E and I were near the end of a giant second line, behind the last brass band. We never got much beyond a buoyant, rhythmic walk ourselves, but there was wild street dancing all around us, ebbing and flowing, hitting truly euphoric peaks. This was mid-July, brilliant sun and sweaty streets. The parade essentially became a mobile party, and stayed that way — a life-celebrating response to death that is the essence of a jazz funeral. Onlookers gathered on the sidewalks to cheer. We ran into people we knew. "Burn, K-Doe, Burn!" people shouted. (This was one of his slogans, but it still seemed like an odd thing to yell, given the circumstances.)

The parade wound its way to Claiborne and stopped at St. Louis Cemetery No. 2 (all the streets on the route had been closed), where the tombs are old and packed together. Weaving between them I was startled to nearly run into a man in a large wig and a blue, polyester suit who looked exactly like K-Doe, except that he was on crutches, on account of a partially missing leg. Later I heard that this was his brother.

I grew up with a particular set of ideas about death, shaped mostly by the desire to hold it at a fearful and ignorant distance. I don't think I can say that these experiences with jazz funerals have changed those ideas in me. But now, at least, I understand that that there are other ideas about mourning that are real and sincerely felt – and that their expression depends in part on a public-ness that might seem to be odds with some notions of grief and loss. Presumably animated by just such a spirit, the celebratory mourners left the cemetery and headed further along Claiborne to the Mother In Law Lounge, to mourn and celebrate some more.

SEPTEMBER 2001

holiday burning

On Christmas Eve Day we drove 35 miles or so upriver to the neighboring towns of Gramercy and Lutcher, in St. James Parish. Both towns abut the Mississippi River levee. All along the levee ridge, here and further upriver to Paulina (about five miles away) and maybe beyond that, stood a series of wooden towers. There were at least a hundred of them, I guess, essentially made as tall and skinny pyramids of stacked wood, rising from a square base to heights of 20 feet or more. We came to see them burn.

Like many inexplicable practices, this one is chalked up to tradition: The lighting of bonfires on the levee has gone on

 for 100 years or more. Every year around Thanksgiving, groups of families and friends get together and start putting these things up, burning them down on Christmas Eve. The poetic explanation is that the flaming towers light the way for Papa Noel. Some sources trace the practice back to French/Cajun settlers, others to German settlers; still others link the whole thing to a Celtic solstice ritual.

Maybe it seems puzzling to keep alive a so-called tradition whose origins are so murky — a link to an unspecific past. But let's not work overtime trying to figure it out: It's cool to watch things burn without serious fear of being harmed in the process. Don't you think?

• • •

So E and I drove up River Road, which runs along the levee, then at Paulina we doubled back and found a place to park in Gramercy. The levee is a man-made hill, its ridge about 20 feet higher than River Road, stretching out like an endless wall between the water and the towns near the water. Heavy rains in states further up the river make its water level rise (it's at an unusually high 13 feet above sea level around New Orleans right now), and without the levee there would be — and there has been — disastrous flooding. So the levee is a central fact of life in the River Parishes, or in any community along the Mississippi, from the Delta to New Orleans.

At the top of the levee is a foot path several feet wide. From there it slopes on either side, at an angle steep enough for children to have a good time rolling down. That's what they were doing on Christmas Eve Day in Gramercy and Lutcher.

We walked the levee and studied the towers close up. A few locals had assembled shapes more ambitious than a simple tower. The volunteer fire department made a huge boat out of logs. There was another log-boat a few hundred feet away. And then there was the cottage.

The cottage — big enough to walk around or lie down in, or to sit on the front porch — was such an impressive structure that we had to compliment its creators. The ringleader identified himself as Reginald, and said he'd been helping make bonfire-fodder pretty much his whole life. He and his crew seemed to be the only black bonfire-makers in the immediate area, and in the big, taped-off area in front of the cottage stood a wooden cutout of a black Mr. & Mrs. Claus, embracing. Reginald showed us pictures of last year's project: a log Impala.

Another year they built a log Superdome. This year they'd made the cottage. We told him it was a shame to think of burning it down. But that's why we built it, he shrugged.

• • •

The sun went down. A riverboat pulled up nearby, and you could see the people milling around inside, waiting for the fires to start. Which they did, at about 7 p.m., as promised. From where we stood, near one of the two log "boats," you could see the pillars of blazing orange, lined up and stretching in a row around the river bend and on out of sight. There was a big, white, stuffed bear in the crow's nest of this log boat. Would they leave him up there?

They left him up there. Like most of the structures on the levee, the log boat was soaked in gasoline, and now its builders were charging around and lighting it up. A boy around five years old helped. In about a minute the whole thing was enveloped in sheets of flame and giving off enough heat to drive me back a few steps. One lick of flame reached the back of the bear's head, which instantly melted away, releasing a snow-like and thoroughly disturbing flurry of bear stuffing. E speculated at the psychological scars such a sight would have left on her, but all the kids around us seemed to be having the time of their lives. Almost every family seemed to have brought along a huge quantity of fireworks, and those were going off now. I crossed over to the river-side levee slope, and in both directions all was smoke and flame and firecracker pops. Indistinct figures (children, mostly) darted around in the haze.

We walked downriver, past the fire department's burning boat (by now it was comforting to think that the fire department was intimately involved in all this) and tower after tower. We could see the burning cottage. As we reached it the fire was in full flower, but the shape of the structure was still intact and recognizable.

I don't have any big theories about why a charming guy like Reginald would take such satisfaction in creating an elaborate structure, and then destroying it, year after year. Any ritualized spectacle that brings friends and relatives together has some appeal, I guess, particularly if it seems unique to a specific community. And maybe all the best traditions are about some quintessentially finite moment (a fire, in this case), repeated infinitely. Just building a new structure every year wouldn't be enough; you have to destroy it, so you can start over. The event is temporary, but its recurrence is permanent.

We waited until the fire made the roof of Reginald's cottage, little by little, collapse in on itself, in a satisfying gush of sparks. I pondered using a picture of a burning cottage on a holiday card — "Hey, it's a *Christmas tradition* around here." Maybe not. One of Reginald's crew tossed Mr. & Mrs. Claus into the blaze. Again we discussed psychological scars. And then we went home.

DECEMBER 2001

letters from new orleans

k-doe

The other day, E and I visited the tomb of Ernie K-Doe, in the middle section of St. Louis Cemetery No. 2. We'd last been here for his funeral.◉ In New Orleans, as you may know, the dead generally aren't buried, because the city is mostly below sea level. Instead the cemeteries are thick with tombs, many of them six feet tall, some of them considerably larger — there is frequently more than one body per tomb, so you can wander through and see by the inscriptions which ones contain husbands and wives or even multiple generations of the same family.

The tomb of Ernest Kador (that's K-Doe's real name) is relatively modest, though it has lately been spruced up a bit.

◉ SEE THE STORY "DEATH AND AFTER."

There's a plaque that identifies him as the "Emperor of the Universe," which is how he referred to himself. It continues: "Along with the 'Star Spangled Banner,' his signature R&B classic 'Mother-In-Law' will be one of only two songs to ultimately be remembered." This, too, is a variation on something that K-Doe said, often. "His wake and funeral," the plaque reads, "comprised the most spectacular send-off New Orleans has ever experienced." Actually, there's some truth in that one.

• • •

Back in the 1950s and early 1960s, Ernie K-Doe had some R&B hits, "Mother-In-Law" (from 1961, written by Allen Touissaint) being the biggest. It still gets played on oldies radio, and if you heard it, you'd recognize it. Like a lot of black musicians from that era, he never really saw a big financial payoff; he faded from the scene, battled alcoholism for a long time, literally wandered the streets in a haze. Later he had a stint as a radio DJ, and would play music between lengthy, erratic soliloquies that focused on himself and his career, and often concluded with the emphatic declaration "I'm cocky, but I'm good!" or the equally spirited self-exhortation, "Burn, K-Doe, burn!" Sometimes that station still plays recordings of these stream-of-conscious monologues, and they're amazing; people actually collect them.

Finally he met and subsequently married a woman named Antoinette, who apparently helped him clean up his act and mount a comeback of sorts. Ernie K-Doe's Mother-In-Law Lounge opened in 1996. It's on a somewhat menacing stretch of Claiborne Avenue, practically under the expressway.◉ A run-down building in a run-down part of town, it's the sort of place you would never stumble across by accident, and even if someone sent you there you might double-check the address. Incongruously, there was generally a big, older, white limo outside, parked on the sidewalk.

We hadn't been in a few months, so we stopped by the other night, but it was closed for the evening and seemed to be undergoing some kind of makeover. This is too bad, and I hope it doesn't change too much, because I really liked the way it looked.

The main room contained a bar, about a dozen old tables, a red-and-blue carpet, all of it looking rather worn. There were many, many photos of K-Doe at all stages of his career, some with Antoinette and her cousin Tee Eva, who sang back-up for him as the Paradise Ladies. There was also a life-sized mural of K-Doe looking beatific. The old K-Doe posters included one promoting a 1950s Dew Drop Inn show. There were also some vague proclamations from the City Council, and a number of fancy parasols hanging upside down from a clothes line. On one visit the decorations included a proposed recording contract that K-Doe found offensive, its pages displayed individually;

◉ THIS STRETCH OF CLAIBORNE IS THE SUBJECT OF THE STORY "UNDER THE FREEWAY."

he went on at great length about this evil document that night. A more recent addition was a mannequin that a local artist transformed into a K-Doe statue, dressed in one of his spangled suits; it contains a tiny transmitter that broadcasts a short, repeating tape loop of K-Doe yelling things like "You *know* you don't look good as I!" and "I *am* the star of New Orleans!" You can hear it at 1500 on your AM dial, if you are within about 50 feet of the statue.

A second and even more worn-out room (later renovated) included a couch and a television set blocked off in the corner. Although almost every time we visited there was loud live music in the front, back here the set was always on, with the sound down, and there was an old, tiny, and nearly bald woman sleeping, or at least lying under covers, on the battered couch, as if a wall had fallen away to reveal some neighbor's private living room. This was Antoinette's mother — that is, Ernie K-Doe's mother in law.

• • •

One night back when K-Doe was still doing his thing, we took our visiting friend Amy to the Mother-In-law. K-Doe has two primary sets of fans. One is made up of young whites — the punk/arty/boho scene. (One of the first times E and I visited the bar, it was to see a tribute show thrown by local punk bands to honor K-Doe, and it was packed. We were standing on the sidewalk when an ambulance pulled up to deal with a guy who had passed out in the gutter. One of the EMS workers took the time to get K-Doe's autograph.) The second set of fans is middle-aged or older, and black.

On this particular night with Amy the crowd was small, and entirely in the latter category. There was no live music. As usual, the door was locked when we arrived, someone had to come and let us in.

K-Doe, of course, was on hand. He moved slowly around the room, and he took our drink order. There was an unbelievable heaviness to his presence when he was not performing. He gave the impression of being about 600 years old, his face a tangle of wrinkles, his eyes slow and distant under an absurd pile of hair and wig. That night he wore a huge fedora, and an excruciatingly loud, checkered suit that I suspect was a bargain. He had on a white shirt and white tie, with gigantic diamond  (well, "diamond") rings, and a flashy stickpin. His fingernails were all an inch long, like claws. He looked nuts.

There was a woman with short hair, in her 50s I guess, singing along at the top of her lungs to R&B from the jukebox. There was a guy in his 50s wearing big glasses and occasionally staring at E and at Amy for long stretches. We sat there and drank, feeling like extras in a Jarmusch movie. People would leave and Antoinette would say: "See you tomorrow."

• • •

Amy and I returned the next night, and almost all the same people were in fact back. Nobody showed us a flicker of recognition. But the crowd was a little bigger, with members of both fan constituencies. We arrived at the same time as a middle-aged party — two men, two women. The men were not dressed any special way. The women were. In particular, one enormous woman was wearing a tight white dress and her hair was all done up with white beads. Very glamorous.

The band consisted of a young guy playing bass; an older man who had no business playing guitar in public but who was fairly glowing with happiness to be doing it; and, in sunglasses and a what looked like a low-end Vegas suit, one Rico Watts, on the keyboards and drum machine. Watts sang standards in a Presleyan voice, his patter full of references to the loneliness of living in a big old house all by yourself, and the temptations of "hoochie-coochie women." K-Doe stood by the door, looking 600, and wearing the exact same outfit as the night before.

Finally he took the stage. By that I mean he moved about four feet from where he'd been standing, to a spot between the tables and the big mural of himself. Something about wrapping one of those clawed hands around the old-style microphone seemed to pump life through his body and out his eyes, which suddenly seemed to be focused on a different middle distance, a brighter one.

"Let's see if y'all remember this one," he said. He opened with "Te-Ta-Te-Ta-Ta." He sounded good. Not great, but pretty good. The guitarist still couldn't really play, but whatever, there was an energy about the proceedings. K-Doe introduced every song as a cultural artifact of earth-shattering importance and meaning — not as a barely remembered tune now little more than a rare flitter on the AM dial, or as noise pumping out of a crazy-looking, no-cover bar in a part of town where it would be unwise to walk half a block after dark. Soon K-Doe was singing "Mother-In-Law." People were smiling. K-Doe's between-song banter never wavered.

"I'm cocky, but I'm good!" he said, six or seven times.

• • •

At a table by a window were five young white people, all probably around age 30. Amy started referring to the three women in the group as the Coyote Ugly Girls. One wore red pants and a cowboy hat. Another wore a skimpy orange shirt and cutoffs. They were on their feet, writhing, shouting. At one point, these three were stationed in different areas of the room, all shimmying like go-go dancers.

They made a big effort to get several of the black women

(but not the men) to dance with them. They were pulling on them, begging. The one in the orange top, who seemed to me to be the one who had ridden this particular train the longest — she looked both brazen and desperate, a party girl just hanging on because she knows there are no party women — this one simply *had* to get the enormous black woman in the white dress and beads into the action. It was killing her. She wouldn't leave the giant woman alone, swiveling her hips in invitation: *Join us, for God's sake, join us.* The woman raised a half smile and waved them off — and then, suddenly, she capitulated.

For thirty seconds or so she danced, not in a half-hearted way, but not quite with abandon either. Then she sat down again, for good.

• • •

The Coyote Ugly crew was harshing my mellow. They were drunk and flashy and obnoxious, and behaved as though they owned the place. On the other hand, did I own the place? No. Besides, what was I enjoying here? K-Doe's music? The spectacle? The ridiculousness? Did the art-punk crowd embrace this vaguely pitiful guy as an elaborate joke? Were the Coyote Ugly Girls part of that joke, or were they in on it? Was I? Was K-Doe? If everyone is in on a joke, is it still a joke?

People were starting to leave. When the black couples departed, they gave a word or a glance to K-Doe, and he acknowledged it with his eyes, even as he plowed through one "million-seller" after another. When the Coyote Ugly crowd left, the gals blew kisses and even bowed, but if K-Doe could see this (and it's a small room) he gave absolutely no indication of it.

He introduced a new song, which he said would succeed where presidents had failed, where the Pope had failed, where Martin Luther King Jr. had failed. "People all over the country gonna be singing this song," K-Doe assured us. The song was about racial harmony.

Here's what I think: If there was any joke attached to the singular phenomenon of K-Doe, he was the *only* one in on it. Here's a guy who created his own reality, simply by believing in it, or at least seeming to. And it worked.

I have no idea where his act ended and some authentic insanity might have begun, but K-Doe had the ability to make a night special, for us, the Coyote Ugly Girls, the bohos, and the middle-aged couples, all at once. Of course the things it says on his tomb are preposterous. On other hand, the plaque is real and the tomb is clean. Recently Antoinette's mother, that woman who used to sit in front of the TV in the other room, passed on; so the tomb of Ernie K-Doe was opened, and now his mother in law rests with him there.

MARCH 2002

masked

Carnival season has a deflationary effect on the news cycle in New Orleans. In the weeks before and the days after Mardi Gras, the stories covered by the newspapers and the evening news are full of familiar features. We hear about hotel occupancy rates, arrest statistics, and announcements about celebrities participating in this or that parade. There are profiles of this season's king and queen of major krewes, Rex and Zulu,◉ and assorted recaps of local traditions. And once it's over and the cleanup begins, there is a tally of how much trash was collected — the depressing barometer the city uses to gauge the relative success of its biggest tourist attraction.

◉ SEE THE STORIES "HIGH SOCIETY" AND "ZULU."

I had a feeling this year would be different, though, when I received an anonymous recorded phone call a few weeks ago attacking one of the candidates in the city's upcoming mayoral election. "Don't be fooled" by Ray Nagin — a Cox Communications cable executive whose mayoral candidacy had just begun to surge — the automated female voice warned me. Despite his outsider talk, the voice continued, Nagin is a tool of outgoing Mayor Marc Morial's "machine"; voters who want a break with the past would be well advised not to support him. The recording didn't suggest who a better candidate might be or give any indication as to who funded this sneak attack. It just ended. I hit *-69 and got a recording saying the call had come from (000) 000-0000.

The Times-Picayune subsequently reported that the mystery calls were carefully targeted to white voters. (Nagin, like most of his mayoral competitors and 67 percent of New Orleans' population, is black). But the paper never determined who was behind them. It was equally hard to figure out which candidates were behind many of the carefully targeted campaign mailings, frequently containing wild allegations of wrongdoing, that marked this year's election. In a city notorious for its inefficiency, political opponents are smeared with dazzling precision.

Days after I received my prerecorded call, Nagin was the surprise top finisher in the first round of voting; last weekend he won the runoff by a solid 59 to 41 margin. It was a fascinating campaign for a relative New Orleans newcomer like me. But even old-timers seemed surprised by the race, which culminated in the town where the good times roll settling on a bona fide businessman as its new leader. The fact that Nagin comes from the not-exactly-populist world of cable is just icing on the King Cake.

The consensus among observers here is that the city is ready for a change, and one can certainly see why that might be. New Orleans has been losing jobs and population for decades; what was once a financial center for the South is today an economic backwater, a punch-line city that's been described as having a business and political culture more Caribbean than American. While cities from Austin to Atlanta have developed whole new economic sectors, here it's all about tourism, oil, and the port, as it has been for years. So you can see why New Orleanians might be ready for a change. Don't get me wrong: I love living in New Orleans. But if my livelihood depended on the local economy, I'd have to move.

Perhaps the most startling thing about the Nagin candidacy is that his entire campaign lasted just about three months. As recently as mid-January, he was registering about 5 percent in the polls, just another face in a field of 15 candidates. Most of the top challengers were political veterans, and the "outsider" vote seemed to be coalescing around Richard Pennington, the police chief. Though Pennington was the early front-runner, he suffered from the perception that he was secretly controlled by Morial — exactly the same charge later leveled against Nagin in those blind phone calls. It was an odd complaint given that Morial is a popular two-term mayor who even now enjoys sky-high approval ratings. Despite this, his attempt to amend the city charter to run for a third term was stomped by voters, whose general feeling about him seems to be, "Marc did a great job, and we want all traces of him removed from public life." The curious upshot was that being endorsed by the well-liked mayor was political anathema, and Morial was duly invisible through the campaign.

Pennington eventually twisted this logic even more. As Nagin gained momentum, the police chief started criticizing him for gaining too much support from influentials who had previously been in Pennington's camp. "I'm glad they're all with you now, because you're stuck with them," he told Nagin in one of their debates. This attempted jujitsu was of a piece with Pennington's entire campaign. First came a radio ad, aimed at black voters, suggesting that Nagin is a closet Republican who supported George W. Bush and ought to be called "Ray Reagan." Weeks later Pennington was running ads prominently featuring praise for his police work from the previously demonized Bush.

Then there were the smears, many of them — like the phone call I received — mysterious in origin. On Lundi Gras, Pennington held a news conference to announce that he had obtained information "that sickens me to my core" concerning Nagin's business practices, which he pronounced "abusive, if not corrupt." It took two more days before he made the more specific (if something short of core-sickening) charge that millionaire Nagin had tried to launch a car-rental business under a program for "disadvantaged" minorities. The mudslinging peaked days later when Pennington accused Nagin of circulating an anonymous letter alleging that the police chief was a wife beater. This sordid turn drowned out the familiar post-Carnival news, which found that though trash tonnage was up, hotel business was "not as robust" as in the past. And, as *The Times-Picayune*'s social columnist enthused, the Mistick Krewe of Comus ball —a surreally anachronistic masked affair that ends the season◉ — once again "served as an apogee of Carnival tradition and excitement."

Watching the mayoral campaign against the Carnival backdrop, it was hard not to dwell on the cliché of New Orleans as a city of masks. The election made it easy to cook up conspiracy theories. Pennington's forked relationship to Bush was just one example of a candidacy that seemed like a study in masking — an impression driven home when he commented just over a week before Election Day that, if he could start over, "I probably would have a little bit more control of my campaign." So who was controlling it? And

◉ SEE THE STORY "HIGH SOCIETY."

what about Nagin? Nothing "sickening" about his business past emerged, but he did fudge facts about whether he was a certified public accountant and whether Morial had helped him to found a local minor-league hockey team. Sure Nagin is charming and seems successful, but what's behind the campaign mask? Was he really in Morial's pocket after all? What would that mean? And who was behind the allegation anyway?

But the most interesting questions are about New Orleans itself. True, the election seemed driven by a hunger for change. And yet the general culture here seems proud and determined to resist change. Mardi Gras is merely the most conspicuous example both of an obsession with tradition and the city marketing itself as, above all else, a unique party environment. The relentless focus on tourism has amounted to New Orleans betting its future on its skill in preserving its past. Can Nagin alter that mindset? Does anybody really want him to?

MARCH 2002

yvonne's

Two things New Orleans doesn't lack for are bars and vacant buildings. There are corner bars in most every neighborhood, and there are blighted little houses and defunct mom-and-pop shops. Sometimes ex-neighborhood stores get converted to homes, but the old signs stay in place, an advertisement for the past. As you drive to our house from Carrolton Avenue you pass several places like this on Dumaine and St. Philip. There's a departed drug store, a long-gone bar called Curly's, the former Murphy's Seafood, and Yvonne's.

Actually, Yvonne's is a special case. When E and I first moved here a couple of years back we noticed Yvonne's and wondered what it had been like, and how long ago it might have closed. Occupying half of a muddy-colored Edwardian shotgun house, it had a beautifully smashed sign hanging over the door touting Jax, a beer that hasn't existed in a long time. There was another Jax sign in one of the windows, which was otherwise blacked out by dense grating in a diamond pattern. A second window was almost completely obscured by a hunk of plywood that had served as a small billboard, but now advertised nothing. I think there was one full letter from the bar's name still floating there, an "n" maybe. The door was right on the corner, its screen ripped and fluttering; you couldn't see inside at all.

Yvonne's sat on one of those informal borders common in many cities: Walk a block in one direction and you're on a wide street with big, clean yards and huge, shady oaks. Walk

 a block the other way and there's no shade, there's trash all over the sidewalks, idle people hang around at all hours on their porches or right in the street itself, sometimes glaring. In the latter direction (two blocks over from our house) there have been at least two murders since we've lived here.

I wish I had a picture of Yvonne's from 2000, but the best I can do is one from 1995, when there was still part of a Newport ad on the billboard; almost all the letters in the bar's

name are still there, and because of the angle you can't really see the broken Jax sign that overhangs the door. Anyway, we'd drive by Yvonne's and we'd wonder what history might have preceded its sad demise. Then we found out that, appearances notwithstanding, Yvonne's was actually a working bar. It had never closed at all.

• • •

Also not long after moving here, we went on a whim to a CD release party for a singer called Myshkin. I was very taken with her music and bought the disc (*Why Do All the Country Girls Leave*). There was a song on it called "Yvonne's Bar." It was, in fact, a song about our Yvonne's.

Partly the song is a painting: the absence of oaks, the ripped-screen door, the children with outdated toys, the houses small and "cut in two" (that is, duplexes, or doubles, as they're called here), the "boys in the street who will give you hard looks." It's a slow and wistful number, the tempo set by Myshkin's rich voice and a plaintive banjo. The song also tells a story about Yvonne herself — how she "died last December" after years spent working lousy jobs to support her three kids, and how the bar has been shuttered for twenty years.

That part, of course, was all made up.

• • •

We'd lived here at least a year before we actually found the nerve to go up to the door of Yvonne's and push, which was literally the only way to figure out if there was truly anything going on inside. Apparently the place opened at about 11 a.m., and usually closed by 5, so we walked over in the daylight with our friend Randy. Sure enough, there were a handful of people inside, drinking in the middle of the day.

It was very dark, and cluttered. Maybe it hadn't been closed for 20 years, but it looked like it had been about that long since anybody made a move toward sprucing things up. The main drink attraction was Budweiser, for one dollar a can. We had some. Video poker machines bleated, and there was a pool table. A woman in late middle age hovered around — Yvonne. It was an odd scene. It felt like three in the morning. It felt illicit. We didn't rush right back, but the idea of this decrepit-looking place with its clutch of secret-society mid-day drinkers became one of my favorite things about the neighborhood.

• • •

Then one fine day I drove past Yvonne's and there was a fresh layer of bright blue paint around walls. That tiny billboard was gone, and so was the mesh grating. You could now see through the windows; the place had been cleared out and the claustrophobic drop ceiling lifted away. Later the word "Pal's" was painted on the windows; tragically, the smashed Jax sign disappeared.

I asked around, and the word was not so good. Neighbors to the bar were worried — the new place was co-owned by a young guy who ran a popular club in the Quarter, and would be open till late. What if  Pal's became a hip spot? Who needed the noise? Who needed the trouble? Later I spoke to someone at the Historic Landmarks Commission, and it turned out that Yvonne's had been rated "architecturally or historically important," and the new alterations were only possible because the bar happened to sit in a part of New Orleans where the rules are a bit lax. In a general way, I jumped on the "I am worried about this" bandwagon, even though I had only been to Yvonne's once. My delightful symbol of timelessly picturesque decay was turning into a trendy bar, and I was agin' it.

• • •

Eventually Pal's opened. We heard no reports of trouble, and within a week we decided to pay a visit. The days of dollar Buds were long gone, of course. The new place sold not just imported beer, but Red Bull. But we had to admit it was nice to have those great, big windows released: The light inside was quite beautiful during the day.

At night, Pal's didn't seem like a throbbing scene, but a fairly warm neighborhood bar. The crowd was younger, mostly neighborhood hipsters. The place was cleaner, with a slightly half-hearted cocktail nation decor. For a while a guy was showing up on Wednesday nights and playing 78s on two old turntables. Lately someone else has been offering manicures ("Manicure & Martini, $5"). The pool table is gone, but of course the video poker is still there, supplemented by an ATM.

The real-life Yvonne, I'm told, simply sold the place and moved to a nearby suburb. A bartender related the story of how the one window came to be covered by plywood: Apparently, years ago, somebody tossed a huge rock through it. The billboard appeared. Maybe this was because the glass was too expensive. Or maybe it was part of a general effort to, in effect, disguise the place, to dig in as the neighborhood went through an earlier, different set of changes — the kind of changes that bring killings and the drug trade and shuttered businesses. The rock, which is about the size of a volleyball, is still there, used from time to time as a door-holder.

I assume some neighbors are still bothered by the place, but E and I stop by from time to time anyway. It's overpriced for the neighborhood, and the "vintage" nude-girl drawings are pretty tedious, but it's the nearest bar. They also don't care if we bring the dog in. It could be worse. Basically, if Pal's is a problem, we're now part of it.

. . .

It's a small story, I know. Just another little outbreak of gentrification, the kind of thing people like me spend half our time complaining about and the other half causing. Possibly because New Orleans resists change so ferociously, often to the city's own detriment, it seems extra sad when it happens anyway. In a lot of ways, the past is all New Orleans has. My favorite line in "Yvonne's Bar" is, "People round here don't know how to let go." That part of the song is true.

Myshkin, I'm sorry to say, will soon be a part of New Orleans' past, too, just like Yvonne's. She's leaving for Portland. We went to her farewell gig the other night at Café Brasil, and it was another fine and surprising show, with one number accompanied by tap-dancing, and another by an outbreak of hula-hooping. A couple of songs into the second set, Myshkin called our friend Ed up to the stage with his banjo, and they played "Yvonne's Bar." It was nice to hear it live one last time.

JUNE 2002

ms. flowers

What about the French Quarter? Don't we ever go there anymore? Of course we do. Just the other night I persuaded E to take a trip to the quarter of the Quarter (the French Sixteenth?) that's most familiar to tourists, and that we normally visit only with out-of-town guests. It's hot and sticky in August and so relatively quiet there — you can park right on Canal Street. The occasion was a performance by John Sinclair, a bona fide underground celebrity who makes his home in New Orleans. But since we had time to kill before he took the stage at the local House of Blues outlet, we also took a chance on seeing another notorious local, Ms. Flowers.

• • •

The Gennifer Flowers Kelsto Club is on St. Louis Street, just river-side of Bourbon, across from Antoine's. We arrived at about 8:30 p.m. and ascertained that there was no cover charge. "It's sort of built into the price of the drinks, if ya know what I mean," the guy working the door said with a grin, in an instance of disconcerting candor.

It's a small place with, at that moment, only a handful of patrons. There's a baby grand piano, painted gold a long time ago and now mostly enclosed by a narrow bar with about eight stools. There are several tables and another bar at the back of the room. The piano bench is backed up to the wall, and on either side are two nice, big windows, flung wide open and facing St. Louis Street. We sat at the piano bar and ordered bourbon.

It was my assumption that we would not see Ms. Flowers. I'd read that she "sings when the mood strikes," and the one time I'd called the bar in the past to see if she was in the house, I was told she "hasn't been in tonight," in a way that suggested to me that she drops by once a month. So as we drank I speculated as to what it might be that Ms. Flowers actually does with her time. Does she summer on the continent? In Arkansas? Plastic stand-up menus on the table turned out to be gee-gaw price lists: We could buy a Gennifer Flowers CD for $10, or a copy of "her" issue of Penthouse for $200. If she showed up, we could get a picture taken with her for $6.

The club opened about a year ago, in a space that's been many things. Most recently it was the local Lucky Cheng's, the Asian, transvestite-waitress restaurant. Way back when it was the Kelsto, a bar with a high-end whorehouse upstairs. As for the main attraction, Ms. Flowers' web site says: "In the time since historic headlines made her a central media figure, the world has come to discover that Gennifer Flowers is a remarkable talent, who doesn't need controversy to make her a star." The site adds that she has appeared on talk shows all over the world, and says that she lectured at Oxford on the subject, "Surviving Sex, Power And Propaganda." She also had a cameo in a Woody Harrelson movie called *Play It to the Bone*.

Now, after living in Little Rock and then Dallas and then Las Vegas, she has moved to New Orleans. The official cultural explanation for this decision is that New Orleans welcomes those whom others might scorn; past sins don't matter in the city that care forgot (source: Rick Bragg in *The New York Times*).

• • •

A few words, then, on notoriety. John Sinclair has it, too. Sinclair was the manager of the MC5, and his 1960s incarnation is described by Fred Goodman in *The Mansion on the Hill* as "poet, marijuana activist, and founder of the youth-oriented White Panther Party." In 1965 he did six months after a drug bust. Later, around the time that the MC5 was putting distance between itself and Sinclair's radicalism, he was convicted for possession of two joints and sentenced to nine and a half years in prison. In December 1971, 15,000 people showed up at a concert/rally for him, headlined by John Lennon and Yoko Ono; Stevie Wonder and Bob Seger, among others, also performed. Sinclair got out a few days later, and paid a visit to The Dakota.

Eventually he moved to New Orleans. I often listen to his radio show on WWOZ; it's devoted to local music, nothing political or revolutionary. His new thing is a cycle of poems about Delta blues legends, which he reads against the backdrop of a live band, in his rocky and bombastic voice. The result is peculiar, because for all the passion and intensity of his delivery, his poems sound a lot like lectures, or even book reports. One number starts with Sinclair stating, "Tommy Johnson, born in Crystal Springs, Mississippi, in 1896, left home around 1912 with an older woman and traveled north to Rolling Fork, then settled farther north in Boyle, by the Dockery Farm, in 1913…" and so on, all over a slinky blues guitar line. Later in that song he recites a minute-long scholarly passage about Legba, the Yoruba god, from Robert Palmer's book Deep Blues. This is what we were going to see him do at the House of Blues, before he and his band, The Blues Scholars, packed up to ride an Amtrak into the Delta and up to Chicago, performing along the way.

The point of all of this is that while John Sinclair is probably the coolest white man in New Orleans, and Gennifer Flowers is essentially the punch line to a bad joke, they do share a certain notoriety (defined broadly), and New Orleans does seem to have served each of them rather well. Sinclair is certainly doing exactly what he wants to do, and Ms. Flowers, well, she claims she's dreamed of being a singer since childhood.

But on the other hand, isn't America in general simply a much easier place to be notorious than ever before? Practically any public "sinner" this side of John Walker Lindh seems welcome to, say, box on Fox, or shill for 1-800-Collect, or whatever. Most of the people at Ms. Flowers' club don't live in New Orleans at all; even in the low season of August the French Sixteenth is just a dirty-Disney fantasyland for middle Americans, and a pocketful of notoriety is just another trinket.

• • •

At the Kelsto Club, a lightly loopy woman who looked to be in her late 50s sat down at the piano and began playing standards and grinning insanely. A middle-aged customer with blow-dried hair and a wide face took the microphone and sang "Smoke Gets in Your Eyes." A passing mule hauling a carriage full of tourists veered toward one of the bar's open windows practically stuck his head in the room. "A Democrat!" the piano player exclaimed. E said to me: "I think we should come here every Friday night. You wear a tuxedo and I'll wear a formal gown. It'll be our eccentricity."

And then, there she was, the zaftig Ms. Flowers, chatting at the bar, wearing a flowing and colorful shawl over a rather low-cut dress (and, E assures me, a well-placed stripe of cleavage-enhancing makeup). And people really did head over to greet her. What did they say? "I must say, I certainly do recognize you." "It's a real honor to be in the presence of someone I've seen on television." "Your general familiarity to me is just wonderful, congratulations on that." I don't know.

Half an hour later, standing by the piano, she sang. Early in the first number, she looked at E, and then at me. We were only a few feet away. She looked at me for what felt like a long time. It seemed rude to avert my eyes, so I sat there staring back, smiling foolishly. This was so unnerving that I can't even remember what the song was. Finally she looked away, and in fact she never looked at us again; when she asked various people where they were from, she skipped us.

A young man from Jackson in a baseball cap that read "Footjoy," seated just to Ms. Flowers' right, interrupted her banter at one point to demand another drink. She signalled the waitress and went back to singing, doing a double-entendre number about being "drilled" by a seven-foot-tall dentist. Her voice is fine, neither embarrassing nor special. I guess she has as much talent as Harry Connick Sr., the Orleans Parish D.A. who has leveraged his son's fame into regular singing gigs, or as much as Dr. Frank Minyard, the city coroner, who plays the trumpet.

Ms. Flowers returned to her patter, doing a practiced shtick about lovelorn couples, such as Ike and Tina Turner and Jim and Tammy Faye Bakker. The guy in the "Footjoy" hat made an impudent remark that I didn't catch, to which Ms. Flowers replied, "I'm gettintothat. Andthisismyshow. Soyoushuddup." Presently she referred to her affair with Bill Clinton before launching into "It Was Just One of Those Things." A passing scruffy man with a bottle of orange juice struck up a conversation through the open window with some tourists from Houston, and ignored Ms. Flowers' efforts to wave him away.

After half an hour, there was a set break. It seemed like the right time to leave, and we darted along the sidewalks that will soon be thronged again with visitors as the weather cools. For no discernable reason, the door guy at the House of Blues gave us our Sinclair tickets for free, and we strolled in right at as he was taking the stage. This is why it's worth going out in August in New Orleans: there's less happening, but what is happening is much easier to manage.

At a table by the door, I noticed, you could buy not just Sinclair's CDs and books, but a reproduction of a poster for the Lennon-headlined concert. I think it cost $30 or so. But there's a difference between this and a head shot of Gennifer Flowers.

Right?

AUGUST 2002

under the freeway

The first time I visited New Orleans, it was on a college road trip from Texas. I remember how Interstate 10 rose as we zagged toward the center of town, and how we seemed to be soaring over the city, looking out at the buildings from 30 feet above the ground. So when we took our exit, it felt as if we were descendeding into New Orleans — and it was pretty scary down there. On one side were abandoned-looking buildings, and on the other a weirdly open area underneath the highway itself, shadowy and surreal after dark, with a surprising number of people walking around. What on earth were they doing under the freeway at night?

Then we took a right, toward the French Quarter, and I basically stopped thinking about it. But the image lingered.

Now I know that the blocks-long stretch of cracked pavement under I-10 along North Claiborne Avenue has a story, and it's one of my favorite things to point out to visitors. Almost any time you drive under I-10 anywhere between say, Canal Street and St. Bernard Ave., there are people hanging around, maybe just on their way somewhere, but occasionally eating, chatting, sometimes even sitting in a lawn chair, or playing dominos. It's bizarre. Because the physical space beneath the Interstate is exactly as appealing as you would guess, which is to say not at all.

But this was not always so.

•　•　•

New Orleans has many spacious avenues that are most remarkable for the very wide strip of ground that separates the two flows of traffic. To call this "the median" is inadequate, because it's area that can be thirty or fifty feet across. So here such strips are called "the neutral ground," and I guess the archetype is the neutral ground on St. Charles Avenue. This is where the streetcar line runs, from Carrolton Avenue all the way to the Quarter. Along with the enormous oak trees, the grassy neutral ground is part of what gives St. Charles such a grandiose feeling. During Carnival, most of the important parades follow a route that leads along a chunk of St. Charles, and by Fat Tuesday the neutral ground has been completely overtaken by virtual encampments of families and friends who set up ladders for better viewing and barbecue pits for better eating.

Also port-a-johns.

In another part of the city the same thing happens on the sprawling neutral ground of Orleans Avenue, where it was once pretty common to see couches and other furniture arrayed for parade-viewing comfort, until the city cracked down on that kind of thing.

Up until 1966, Claiborne Avenue also had a very pretty and park-like neutral ground. It was about 10 blocks long and 100 feet across, totaling 13 and a half acres, lined with two rows of mature live oak trees, around 250 of them altogether.

It so happens that the two neighborhoods bisected by this particular public space were Treme and the Seventh Ward, which were, it also happens, predominantly black. Claiborne was lined with businesses and residences, largely one or two-story wood-frame structures from the 19th and early 20th century, and largely black-owned. In the pre-Civil Rights era, black revelers weren't particularly welcome to the uptown Carnival parade celebrations, and thus many celebrated Mardi Gras on Claiborne. The famous Mardi Gras Indians, one of the iconic images of New Orleans today,◉ were a main attraction.

◉ SEE THE STORY "GOLDEN ARROW."

Daniel Samuels, who studied the area as part of his graduate work at the University of New Orleans, wrote in his thesis that North Claiborne was "the locus of cultural and economic life for New Orleanians of African descent."

I thought it would be interesting to look back at the newspaper accounts from the 1960s about the pitched battle that must have been fought over the decision to erase a place of vital importance to a community that has done so much to shape the city's character. What I found was nothing. There was no dramatic public battle. I'm sure people objected, but in those days they were easily ignored. It also seems that many area residents didn't know what was going to happen until the demolition and "tree removal" process began in August 1966. The city's planning commission, according to Samuels, had already concluded that the North Claiborne area showed "existence of severe blight" — they should see it now! — and apparently the thinking was that no one would be harmed or damaged by running a highway through here.

No one who mattered, anyway.

• • •

I wish I could pretend that all of this is truly remarkable, but I'm afraid that if you know anything at all about the way cities have developed in the U.S. in the past 50 or 60 years, you have a pretty good idea that the various sacred grounds of impoverished urban-dwellers have been paved over or otherwise obliterated with some regularity.

What is remarkable about the former Claiborne neutral ground is that it is still used as a public space. I don't mean in any formal way. And I certainly don't mean to suggest that the area, with litter and broken glass on the ground and the claustrophobic roar of cars overhead, is anything like the "promenade" that long-time area residents described to Samuels.

But I myself have been under the freeway many times. I've followed jazz funeral parades on routes underneath it (the acoustics, actually, are fantastic), and I've hung around on Mardi Gras day and at other times when the Indians gather. This past Mardi Gras, E and I watched as a Mardi Gras Indian dance at Claiborne and Esplanade spilled into the street itself, bringing traffic to a complete halt. One unfortunate woman began blaring her horn, and was informed by several onlookers that she was in the wrong place, on the wrong day, to be doing anything like that. An area civics organization called Tambourine and Fan has devoted itself to a mission described succinctly on a banner that fluttered

from the freeway over the corner of Claiborne and Orleans: "Bring Mardi Gras Back to North Claiborne."

• • •

Most of the time the space is used in more quotidian ways. The other day I rode my bike down, and the first thing I saw was an older black man sitting on a little ledge around one of the massive columns that hold the freeway up, eating his lunch. Just like a picnic in the park. Only under the freeway. Most of the people walking, biking, or sitting under I-10 are black (the demographics of Treme and the Seventh Ward haven't changed much), and many look old enough to remember when this space was grass and oaks.

I wanted to take some pictures of a somewhat recent public arts project that aims, I guess, to at least make a public acknowledgment of what this area used to be: A number of support columns have been painted with wraparound murals.

The columns on the outer edges have renditions of oak trees (painted by prisoners, it turns out). Other murals were done by various local artists, with varying degrees of technical skill. Some have celebratory themes — a parading brass band on one, Mardi Gras Indian on another. Some celebrate achievements — the city's first black surgeon, a family that has produced two mayors. And other murals depict slavery, police brutality, and lynching.

I have some copies of pre-1966 photographs of North Claiborne that I got from The Williams Research Center (they asked me not to reproduce these), and I was especially interested in what was still standing from two photos taken at the corner of Claiborne and Ursulines in 1947. In the pictures there are some cool old signs, one for ACME Life Insurance, and another, shaped like a huge paintbrush, for a hardware store.

What's there now is a freeway ramp.

So I rode on. A lot of this space is used for parking, especially near the corner of St. Bernard, where Circle Foods actually looks a lot like it did in a picture I have from 1954. Except of course that the presence of the hulking freeway, and the dearth of other businesses nearby, makes it seem more menacing today. (Samuels found 130 business were listed on this stretch in 1960, and 35 in 2000).

I took some more pictures. It's a nice thought, I guess, painting these columns, but the net effect is pretty depressing. It doesn't mitigate the loss, it underscores it. Although that has value, too.

• • •

Not all the columns are painted, and I noticed one that seemed to have newspaper clippings pasted on it in a little cluster. They were death notices from the local paper (*The Times-Picayune* runs at least a thumbnail obit for pretty much everyone who dies in New Orleans). A guy sitting in his car about 40 feet

 away waved and motioned me over. He was an older black man, missing a lot of teeth, wearing sunglasses and a black cap. As far as I can tell he was just hanging out in his car; maybe he was waiting for someone shopping at Circle Foods, but he was parked an inconvenient distance from there, or from anything else. He rolled his window down and said he'd seen me looking at the obituary column.

"Yes," I said.

"You know any of the people on there?"

"Not really," I said. "I saw the one for K-Doe's mother in law. ◉ Are those all people from the neighborhood?"

"That's right. My sister's up there." He was smiling through all of this, very pleasant and friendly.

I said: "Oh. Who, uh, who puts them up?"

He said someone's name — Chuck, I think — and pointed at a house, as if I would know Chuck who lives across the way there. I said I thought it seemed like a very nice idea, and he said he thought so too, and that he had enjoyed speaking with me. He rolled up his window.

Somehow pasting obituaries to a highway support column says more, to me, than the murals do. My point here isn't to

◉ SEE THE STORY "K-DOE."

romanticize these neighborhoods, or to condemn the decision to slash an interstate through them. I'm neither sentimental nor angry about North Claiborne. But I am somewhat awestruck.

• • •

We all know how a place can have a hold on us, how a patch of earth, a strip of land, a corner, a building, or the most arbitrarily bordered swath of territory you can imagine, can have a symbolic meaning. But surely even that meaning has its outer limits, right? If someone knocks down the building or paves over the land, how can the significance of the place where something used to be hold on to its significance?

Often, I think, the answer is: It doesn't. But sometimes it does. This is not because Symbolic Importance comes bubbling up out of the ground like a hot spring. In fact the meaning doesn't flow from places to people at all; it's actually the other way around. That's the only way the specialness of a place survives the most violent changes in its physical aspect. You can't impose this, but you can't thwart it, either. All you can do is admire it. And you should.

NOVEMBER 2002

luncheon

In most places, taking a long, boozy lunch on a weekday is a rare indulgence, or just flat-out irresponsible behavior. Here in New Orleans it's tradition. This makes sense: New Orleans is big on both tradition and on goofing off while the rest of the world gets things done, so why not combine the two ideas whenever possible?

Consider this passage praising "*the* Friday Lunch," from a recent restaurant review in a local weekly: "Dedicated locals award this ritual the respect of a sacrament. ... The customary etiquette of restaurant dining slackens on Friday afternoons; it's fashionable to wear hats (while eating), it's acceptable to linger (for hours) and it's expected that you'll drink (quite a lot)." The point is to have "a good time, which is the real reason so many New Orleanians play hooky in restaurants on Friday afternoons while the rest of the country golfs."

Actually, the rest of the country doesn't golf, it works. And in some cases it even wonders why it can't get in touch with anyone in New Orleans. But whatever.

The ultimate setting for a "traditional" Friday lunch is Galatoire's. We have known this for some time — they practically tell you about Galatoire's at the airport — but somehow E and I had not had a chance to experience it first-hand until recently.

• • •

Galatoire's is a big deal in New Orleans. How big? This summer *The Times-Picayune* ran a story about how the restaurant had fired a popular waiter, and how some regular customers were upset about it. The story was more than 3,600 words long. It attracted more mail to the paper than any subject since September 11. And it inspired a local theatrical production that sold out several weeks at $16 a ticket.

At the center of the controversy was a man with the aston-ishing name of Gilberto Eyzaguirre. Gilberto (everyone calls him by his first name) is a waiter. At Galatoire's over a period of twenty-some years he built a following. Then he was fired, after two female employees of the restaurant filed sexual harassment complaints against him.

Various patrons of the restaurant, apparently unconcerned about the allegations, thought this firing was a terrible idea, and some 123 of them wrote letters of protest. These were presented, in a bound volume no less, to Galatoire's management. They were also posted on a web site, www.welovegilberto.com. The protestors included local figures like former U.S. Attorney Harry Rosenberg; historian David Culbert; singer John Boutte; journalist Curtis Wilkie; and novelist Richard Ford. A man named Brobson Lutz recounted his unsuccessful attempt at returning to the restaurant, post-Gilberto: "As the evening approached, I just couldn't go. I was afraid I would start crying." His colleagues went without him, and he "ended up eating alone" at another restaurant, "crying into a couple of Martinis."

Well! Obviously the firing touched a nerve. The underlying story, as *The Times-Picayune* described it, was that the Gilberto Incident was the last straw for patrons who thought the restaurant had changed for the worse over the past five years. That's when the Galatoire family, which has run the place since 1905, brought in its first manager who is not a blood relation. One sample complaint: Galatoire's has switched from hand-chopped ice to the kind that's made by a machine. Also the dress code has gotten lax, less-fancy napkins have come into use, and an upstairs dining room was renovated.

Mickey Easterling, in a three-page, all-cap letter, groused that she'd been in with some friends and spent "the better part of $1000" on a lunch marking her daughter's birthday, and the wait staff placed the white wine, red wine, and champagne glasses "helter/skelter...with no rhyme or reason." She added that the "female bartender" upstairs is often "more drunk than your customers." (Which is saying something.) Another three-page letter, from "scholar of Southern literature" W. Kenneth Holditch, read in part: "People who seem to be arrayed to go to the beach or Disneyland, wearing blue jeans and sweatshirts or worse, are ushered in to be seated next to a table where some well-dressed elderly couple, long-time patrons, sit, mourning the passing of a more gracious era....Not only is tradition difficult to establish, but once lost or destroyed, it can never be regained. Do you really want the traditions of your historic establishment to be swept out by a new wave of clueless youth? ...Do we want to drive away the customers, many of them descendants of men and women known to our ancestors, to be replaced by tourists from Iowa and Indiana in jeans, halter tops, and sandals?"

A few weeks after *The Times-Picayune* story, there was an incident during Friday lunch at Galatoire's. This incident also made the paper: "Two slender and well-dressed men, unsmiling and wearing dark sunglasses, burst into the door of the restaurant and released a hundred helium-filled white balloons emblazoned with 'welovegilberto.com.'"

. . .

A lot of people who do not happen to be part of the New Orleans blue-blood crowd thought that all of this was pretty silly. And possibly embarrassing. And certainly funny. The 123 letters became the basis of a little show called "The Galatoire Monologues," overseen by local newspaper columnist and sometime performer Chris Rose. We attended one of the shows, in which local actors and personalities read from the letters for laughs. Highlights included a drunk-sounding Davis Rogan (a local DJ and musician) singing Richard Ford's letter to his own bluesy, bleary, piano accompaniment. Oddly, Brobson Lutz, the guy who cried into his martini, also turned up as one of the reader/performers.

I assumed everyone at the downtown club performance would be a hipster ironist out to guffaw at the expense of the stuffed-shirt Galatoire crowd. But at least half of the audience *was* the Galatoire crowd, sitting primly in their proper ensembles and having a perfectly delightful evening. The We Love Gilberto site even touted the show. I checked around and found that Gilberto himself had come to several performances, and was treated (or at least behaved) like a celebrity. (Dept. of New Orleans is a Small Place, Part One: Gilberto has since found employ at a restaurant that happens to be operated by our next-door neighbors.) One person loosely connected with the performance told me that the wayward waiter also hit on all the cocktail waitresses at the club. I checked that with someone else in a position to know, who confirmed it and said that he hit on customers, too. Meanwhile, I am told the brouhaha has actually boosted business for both Galatoire's and for Gilberto's new employer.

• • •

Seizing my last opportunity to be considered part of "a wave of clueless youth," I agreed with E that the time had come to eat at Galatoire's. It would be Friday lunch, downstairs where the traditionalists sit, or it would be nothing. Of course you can't make a reservation for this, so we planned to arrive at 11 a.m. Unfortunately we'd chosen a Friday in the busy season. By 11 a.m. all the downstairs tables had been spoken for by people who'd come as early as 8. (Sometimes regulars actually hire placeholders to stand in line for them, or so I've read.) So we got on the list and prepared for an estimated two-hour wait. We walked around the French Quarter for a while, E bought a book, and I gradually got tense about the various editors I was ducking. We went back to Galatoire's to wait at the bar. Another tradition at the restaurant is the mixing of very strong drinks, and my gin seemed to have been only lightly splashed with tonic. Okay.

We waited. There were, in fact, an incredible number of silly hats on the heads of silly women. The bar was very crowded, and everyone was drinking. (Dept. of New Orleans is a Small Place, Part Two: A bartender from Pal's⦿ was there and wearing an *extremely* silly hat.) We waited a long time. I got tense again. We kept checking the list downstairs. We decided that the schlumpy kid with the cell phone was one of those hired place-holders. E began reading *The Wind Done Gone* to pass the time.

It was 2:30 or so when we were finally seated. The dining room was cacophonous. Our waiter, "Reynard," could sense that we weren't in a great mood at this point, and labored to cheer us up. What cheered us up was the crowd. I was facing a table of six or eight people who seemed to have finished their main courses but had no plans to move. They were carrying on. One woman with a lot of makeup wore a form-fitting, off-the-shoulder, red dress; its trim was a wide band of fur, with at least three little mink heads peering out of it. Actual heads.

Lots of people were table-hopping. At one point a male friend of the mink-head lady came over to greet her, and as they stood with their backs to us, their arms around each other, we watched her hand get more and more adventurous in which part of his body she squeezed. He squeezed back. (Dept. of

⦿ PAL'S IS EXPLAINED IN THE STORY "YVONNE'S."

New Orleans is a Small Place, Part Three: This man was E's dermatologist. His face was very smooth.)

Eventually we started to notice that a lot of the tables around us were filled with people who had apparently finished eating. None of them made the slightest effort to move. (Except for that schlumpy cell-phone kid — he left after the people who had apparently hired him got seated.) People ordered more champagne, or even another round of food, and carried on. E and I soldiered through our courses as if in a parallel universe. (Obligatory food comment: everything was fine, but the only true standout was the oysters en brochette appetizer ordered by E.) It was getting close to 4 o'clock, which meant there was at least one editor who was likely to be extremely concerned as to where I might have been for the past *five hours*. Obviously the idea at Galatoire's really is just to stay indefinitely — but, really, how can so many people be in a position to simply check out for the better part of a weekday?

That's the thing about tradition: It obliterates such pesky questions. It obliterates *all* questions. Tradition is not the opposite of progress, it is the opposite of reflection: When you have it, when you embrace it, you don't have to worry about consequences or anything else, because tradition fiercely preserved is truly an end in itself.

Through the gauzy curtains we could just make out Bourbon Street and confirm the existence of sunshine and an outside world. But nobody around us was looking out the window. They were walking about in hats and ordering more champagne. Just then Reynard stopped by our table with his humongous smile, and I asked him to bring the check.

JANUARY 2003

bohemians and galatoire's:
a proposal

This summer, two stories dominated local headlines and water-cooler talk for weeks. First was the battle of Galatoire's, wherein the ladies and gentlemen of the Church of Four Hour Friday Lunches, Galatoire's Branch, sent up a howl heard 'round the world over the firing of their favorite waiter — the last straw, they complained, in a series of indignities foisted on them by whippersnapper management. Then came the great bohemian brouhaha, with mainstream media and certified eccentrics alike decrying an academic study that found New Orleans to be merely the 49th weirdest city in America — placing well behind such questionable bohemian havens as Salt Lake City and Dallas.

The two stories seem worlds apart, but they aren't. In fact they're both about the same thing. The impolite way to say it is that both stories are about New Orleans bemoaning the wider world's failure to love the city for what it is. The polite way is to say both stories are about nonconformity — that ingrained refusal of this city to be like any other place, no matter how much the world changes.

What those long-time Galatoire's customers want is for things to carry on just as they always have. With no concession to advances in ice-chipping technology, or changing dress codes. And in the case of some patrons, without any concession to rights that women in the workplace have acquired in, oh, the past seventy or eighty years.

What the advocates of New Orleans as a bohemian enclave basically seem to want is a round of applause. And they do have a point — if you're looking for a city where you don't have to play by the conventions of society, this is a good one. The irony of their ire is that it's focused on a book that celebrates weirdness as a keystone of economic development. The Rise of The Creative Class, by Carnegie Mellon professor Richard Florida, argues that cities like Austin and San Francisco have flourished precisely because of their tolerance for cultural outsiders.

Which brings me to my proposal for economic development in the Crescent City. Maybe what New Orleans needs to do is work harder at bringing together those who have money with the people who have creative ideas that need funding. How about this for a start — "Take a Bohemian to Lunch Day," at Galatoire's.

I guess it might sound like a recipe for mayhem to bring together the city's best-connected and its most outrageous over a big multi-martini lunch. But that's the whole point. If the drinks are mixed strongly enough, maybe all those differences will fade away in a pleasant haze of love for New Orleans, and new plans can be hatched for making this a city with more jobs and more momentum — but still a healthy dose of that specialness that both tribes are in love with.

AUGUST 2003

high society

A year or two ago I was reading a book called *The American Idea of Success*. It was written by Richard M. Huber, and first published in 1971. As the title suggests, it's a history of this country's ideas about how success is defined. I was surprised to find on page 31 a passage indicating that the book would be about success as it's defined in most of America: "This study has excluded the South for good reasons." The big one seemed to be this: "With its romantic enchantment with the past and reverence for family background, the South refused to exalt...the self-raised man."

This isn't the place to debate the merits of that argument, in 1971 or today. And while I have no idea what the quintessential Southern city might be, I am certain it's not New Orleans. But I was reminded of this passage recently during the quintessential New Orleans event, which of course is Carnival.

• • •

The truth is that Mardi Gras was pretty weak this year. The weather was bad and the crowds were noticeably lighter than usual. As is our habit, we took in the day on bikes, riding first uptown, then circling back to the French Quarter, then to Treme. Later we switched to the car and drove down to Frenchmen Street and finally back into the Quarter. There were some highlights here and there. There are always a lot of nutty costumes, we got several good parade looks, we had some excellent treats called callas at a friend's place in Treme, and the nighttime scene on Frenchmen was pretty cool, complete with a spooky power outage. By the time we went down there we had decided to put on our skeleton masks from a parade we marched in a couple of years back. Anyway, I wasn't actually so interested in what happened on the street this year. I was trying to figure out something I could only observe from a distance, which is what Carnival means to the "society" crowd. This has always been a bit of a puzzle to me.

For these people, the season begins on Twelfth Night —

January 6 (the twelfth night after Christmas). Like all the major dates of Carnival season, Twelfth Night is tied to the Catholic calendar: It's the Feast of the Epiphany. Mardi Gras itself is of course Fat Tuesday, the last day before Lent begins on Ash Wednesday. In reality, the religious dimension of the season is basically irrelevant. But a lot of people throw informal Twelfth Night parties, and that night is the also first in what develops into a barrage of debutante and masked balls. Nell Nolan, the society columnist for *The Times-Picayune*, covers them all. She described the guests gathering at the Municipal Auditorium for the ball of The Twelfth Night Revelers, where the question on everyone's mind was, "Who would receive the golden bean?"

I've been reading about this golden-bean business for several years now, but I still don't exactly get it. Apparently a huge cake is presented, with slices given to the young ladies. One slice has a golden bean in it, and some others have silver beans. The young lady who received the golden bean "would wear the accoutrements of royalty," as Nolan put it. The silver-bean-getters are "honored as maids." This tradition apparently goes back to 1870. I guess this is handled in some symbolic way, since Nolan's account makes it clear that the queen has actually been picked before the ball starts.

The king of this ball is a grown man wearing tights, a big sequined cape, a gaudy crown, and a mask. His identity is secret. Judging by the photos in the paper, all of the adult males at the ball wore masks, and what appear to chef hats. In general the masks are strips of white cloth with eyeholes cut in them. So if you're flipping quickly through the paper, you see a page of photos that on first glance appear to show very young women in fancy white dresses, posing with Klansmen. It's a little creepy.

• • •

The social season begins to climax on Lundi Gras (Fat Monday), when we all get to find out who is the queen of the Krewe of Rex, and thus of Carnival itself. When I say, "we all get to find out," you might think I'm kidding, but in fact the announcement is treated like a news event — front page news, in fact. The king and queen of carnival are interviewed on all the local news stations. The paper runs big above-the-fold pictures on A1, plus profiles inside, of "His Majesty Rex and the Queen of Carnival" on the morning of Mardi Gras.

This year Rex was Richard W. Freeman, Jr., who commented to the paper: "It never occurred to me that this would be an honor that I'd receive." Really? His brother Louis was Rex in 1999. His father was Rex. His grandfather was Rex. Freeman is 64 and retired. He used to work for the Louisiana Coca-Cola Bottling Company, which happens to have been founded by his grandfather.

The king is always a man of mature years. "His queen," as the accepted terminology has it, is always a college-age debutante type. This year it was Shelby Scott Westfeldt. She says that when her father told her she would be queen, she burst into tears. Her great-grandfather was Rex. Her mother was queen of carnival, and so was her aunt. Her parents, Uptown plantation-style house has been in the family for five generations.

As I read up on Shelby Scott Westfeldt, I noticed something odd. Although the profile didn't mention it, she was also in the courts of several other organizations this year. At the Proteus ball, she was a maid; ditto the Momus ball, and the Atlanteans ball. She even got a silver bean at Twelfth Night. Perhaps she is one of the most extraordinary debutantes in New Orleans' history, or perhaps there are not enough of these young ladies to go around.

In any case, the vast majority of the city's population could not care less about which interchangeable member of the city's upper crust has achieved "royalty" in any given year.

• • •

And yet…whether the masses are paying attention or not, the society crowd not only perpetuates Carnival, but uses Carnival as the centerpiece of a process by which it perpetuates itself.

In 1857, ninety New Orleans men founded the Mystick Krewe of Comus, and on the night of February 24 (Fat Tuesday) they presented to a curious public a small, two-hour parade, consisting of a pair of floats, masked marchers, and bands. Light was provided by black men carrying elaborate torches. Afterwards was a bal masque, and a banquet for krewe members that ended in the wee small hours of Ash Wednesday. There is more, endlessly more, to be said about antecedents, from the Mardi Gras parades of Mobile, Alabama, to the earlier celebrations in New Orleans (which included both private masked balls for the leisure class as well as the drunken street antics of the riffraff). But the appearance of Comus set the pattern for Carnival in New Orleans to this day: The city's elite provides the masses with a free spectacle, then retreats to private parties.

Today there are dozens of parades, starting almost two weeks before Fat Tuesday, each put together and underwritten by private krewes. There are no corporate sponsors. Also, The Mystick Krewe of Comus is still around, and that is still what it is called.

The other major "old-line" krewes are Momus, Proteus, and of course Rex. Obviously there are lots of others, and almost all of them have silly names, but I mention those in particular because Comus and Momus don't actually parade anymore.

In the early 1990s, a member of the city council started a ruckus by arguing that the prestige krewes were all-white organizations, New Orleans is a majority black city, and that these guys ought to step into the 20th century and integrate their organizations or they should be denied parade permits. ◉ The council's demand was finally watered down to the point that all the krewes did not have to integrate, or even prove that they didn't discriminate; they merely had to *say* that they didn't discriminate. Rex and Proteus finally went along. Comus and Momus refused, and have not paraded since.

In the middle of the controversy, a local guy who is famous for his "reverence" for Carnival traditions, Henri Schindler, led a parade to the door of the Boston Club, probably the city's most exclusive. Dressed as "King Sarcophagus," he read a florid proclamation on behalf of the quitter krewes, which ended, "Adieu, fair city, until the coming of some happy day when the Furies are done and the Fates call us to ride again to greet you." Then for good measure he threatened the City Hall "junta" that was "sucking the lifeblood of our carnival" with the less-than-artful taunt, "Your days are numbered!"

• • •

The Rex ball is televised. We have watched it. It goes on for hours and hours, and almost nothing happens. It makes you long for a golf tournament. The most interesting thing about it is the grown men in the goofy costumes. The second most interesting thing is the absurd commentary from the society worshippers who "cover" the event (one of these is Schindler), and who

◉ THE MAJOR BLACK KREWE IS DISCUSSED IN THE STORY "ZULU."

never seem to lose their enthusiasm for the word "pageantry." Still, I would like attend this ball, mostly so that I could ask the king whether he and "his queen" have any, you know, *special plans* for later on.

The big highlight of the evening comes when the king of Comus sends a minion to the Rex ball, who invites Rex and his date over to the Comus ball. (This is easily done because the two events are actually held in different parts of the same building.) They always accept. The subtext here is that Comus — despite what any city council naysayers might have thought — is more important than Rex. The identity of the king of Comus is a secret. I am looking now at the pictures published in the newspaper of the Comus ball, and all I can tell you is that he is a short, stout man in a grinning mask and a pageboy wig. There are many pictures of debutantes being squired by men in masks. They are all interchangeable. But I gather that this is the point.

Nell Nolan prounced the event "A crowd pleaser!" She went on to describe the evening's climax — it is the same climax every year. First "the four monarchs and their entourages circle the white canvas-covered floor at the Comus masked ball. Then the royal foursome took their paces on the throne to acknowledge their rapt subjects." The acknowledgement consists of the slow, synchronized waving of three wands and a goblet (Comus gets the goblet), over and over and over and over, all night.

The important thing to remember is that these people are supposed to be the elite of New Orleans. That status — and this is what made me think of that book about the success idea — is emphatically not the status of the "self-raised man." The basic transaction seems to be that these aristocrats give us all the gift of Carnival, and in return they get to play dress-up, and belong to exclusive clubs. Their goal is not to recognize and welcome new members into their society; their goal is to protect what they have. In the guise of upholding the past, they live in the past. This is the classic logic of aristocracy.

Sometimes I think this is funny, and sometimes I think it's sad, because New Orleans is, emphatically, not a city that can afford an aristocracy. And it almost goes without saying that the romantic past they honor is highly selective — its better points exaggerated, its worse aspects ignored, until it becomes a comfortable fiction. And so it is that the more such people succeed in convincing themselves that they matter, the less they really do.

the desire line

On Sundays, Doris Barber and her husband would catch the bus in Central City and ride for 45 minutes or so out to Desire Street. What they looked at when they arrived was construction: a cleared expanse of land where a public housing development would sit. The couple had four children, and a fifth on the way. In Central City they had a one-and-a-half bedroom house, and in the pre-Civil Rights era, as a black, low-income, family, they had few alternate housing options. Today Barber is 71, with a pious demeanor and a remarkably specific memory: July 25, 1956, she says, was the day that she and her family moved into a three-bedroom apartment in the Desire public housing complex. She describes spacious rooms with hardwood floors, and grounds that were manicured and lined with trees and shrubbery. Her neighbors — the complex was always overwhelmingly African-American — were as happy to be there as she was. "Excuse me for the phrase that I'm fixing to say," she adds carefully. "I tell everybody it was like I was moving out of hell into heaven."

Half a century on, there is nothing heavenly about housing projects in New Orleans or anyplace else: Synonymous with crime, drugs, vandalism, and gangs, they are being demolished across the country. The surprising thing about Desire is not that it may once have been beautiful, or that it subsequently slid into despair, but rather that Barber, and 13 other families, simply refuse to leave it.

Or what's left of it. Today heavy work trucks crawl across these 98.5 acres; the building that Barber and her husband first moved into has been bulldozed, like almost every other structure that made up the 1,860-unit Desire projects. The streetcar named Desire stopped running decades ago, but you can still catch a bus that follows the Desire line out here. Not that there is much left to see, except for the three, two-story brick-façade buildings where Barber and her neighbors still live, surrounded by a big, torn-up field.

• • •

Deborah Davis moved into Desire when she was 2 years old, and she lives there still. She is now 48 and has four sons

— 34, 31, 21, and 18 — two of whom live with her. I met with her in one of the last Desire buildings, at 3733 Pleasure Street. Desire, unlike several other public housing complexes in New Orleans, sits on land well outside the city's core, hidden away between a truck route, railroad tracks, and a Superfund site. (This is one of the bleakest sections of a city that has more than its share of poverty and blight, but the street names tell a more optimistic story: Desire Street also intersects Industry, Abundance, Benefit, and Humanity, and runs parallel to Piety.)

I was a few minutes early, and wasn't immediately certain that I was in the right place, because most of the windows were boarded up, and the only signs of life were the trucks rolling past, their drivers looking quizzically at the white guy in a Banana Republic jacket tapping on his cell phone on this particular edge of town. As I waited in the cold drizzle, I wondered, of course, why anyone would put up a fight to live here.

I am not the only one to wonder. The small cohort of the living among the ghostly ruins of Desire is taken here as either a puzzle or an outrage. They are not here by way of inertia; they have fought for this — winning a court decision in August 2002, in fact, that forced the housing authority to spend $200,000 to fix up units it fully intends to raze in a year's time. "While a sentimental attachment to their apartments can be understood," the New Orleans *Times-Picayune* editorial page said of the

Desire tenants at the time, "their determination to stay put and not even leave temporarily is maddening."

Even fellow tenants were skeptical of the decision by Davis (who is president of the Desire Area Residents Council), Barber, and others to defy the eviction notices that arrived in the summer of 2001. Nevertheless, Davis says, in her delicate, singsong voice, "There was never a doubt in our minds." She is an interesting presence: Even-keeled and well-dressed, in a pattern sweater and a beige topcoat, she smiles a lot, even when her observations are grim, or when she is clearly exasperated or angry. "We tried to encourage residents not to leave. But the housing authority at that time had made [getting out] sound delightful. They figured they had a better deal."

The first plan to "revitalize" Desire by razing some buildings and renovating the others was announced in 1991. What happened next was nothing. The start date was pushed from September 1992 to March 1993. Three months after that a Housing and Urban Development official said the revitalization might start "soon." Residents, says Davis, began moving out. "A few left because of the insane conditions we were living in. Others left because they were told they would be able to come back after the units were restored," she says.

As early as the end of the 1970s, and certainly by the start of the 1990s, public housing had taken on the reputation as a dangerous concentration of social pathology, crime, and hopelessness. It was not always this way. The earliest public housing in the United States came about through the Public Works Administration, a product of the New Deal. From 1933 to 1937, the PWA built 25,000 units that were intended to help the battered Depression-era working class escape the slums at a time when the private market, on its own, was not meeting the need for low-cost housing.

Subsequent legislation shifted both the goals and the methods of public housing. On-the-ground responsibility shifted from the federal government to local housing authorities that relied on federal funds. Intellectually, public housing began to be seen as a last resort, a view that would gradually create the kinds of projects that were seen as little more than ware-houses for the poor. A 1949 program gave $300 million to public housing authorities to clear inner-city slums and build ever-bigger projects, including high-rises, throughout the 1950s and 1960s. Desire, though not a high-rise, was part of this wave, with 1,860 units in a sprawl of 40 two-story buildings

Over the eight years of the Reagan era, HUD funding for housing programs was cut by 76 percent and projects all over the country slid deeper into disrepair. In an attempt to keep public housing from simply being choked out of existence by a dearth of money, the Democrat-controlled Congress of 1987 passed a law mandating that torn-down housing units be replaced on a one-for-one basis with new, low-income housing.

This ultimately created a stalemate, and in the absence of new appropriations, projects like Desire were simply left to decay.

The one-for-one rule was done away with in the mid 1990s, opening the door for change but also creating fresh tension. On one side was pressure to do something about housing that was nearly unlivable, and to do it as quickly as possible. And on the other side was pressure to figure out what to do about the tens of thousands of people who were living in it, a process involving massive, time-consuming case management and oversight.

By the early 1990s public housing was particularly grim in New Orleans. In 1979, HUD had devised a system for evaluating the performance of local housing authorities, and the Housing Authority of New Orleans (HANO) was among those designated "troubled." In 1988, HUD revised its agreement with HANO to give the federal agency more oversight of persistent "operational and managerial deficiencies related to poor maintenance of the housing stock."

While Desire waited, a new government program called HOPE VI was hatched. Acting in part on recommendations from the National Commission on Severely Distressed Public Housing, Congress earmarked funds for housing authorities to use for "demolition" and "revitalization" of some properties. The overarching goal was to replace the high-concentration centers of poverty that some projects have become with a combination of lower-density housing, mixed-income developments, and programs that would help former residents get affordable housing in better neighborhoods.

Desire was one of the first Hope VI grant winners, receiving a $44.2 million award from HUD in 1994. The city cancelled its renovation plan up to that point — which had envisioned 1,150 rebuilt or refurbished units — and essentially started from scratch. Little work had been done, apart from some asbestos removal from a few buildings. Eventually a new plan was settled on, calling for most of Desire to be razed and rebuilt, ending up with about 800 units of single-family townhouse-style dwellings.

· · ·

When Davis talks about that period from the early to mid 1990s, there is very little of the nostalgia that her neighbor Doris Barber professes to feel for the 1950s version of the complex. Davis' own childhood memories include police officers hitting female residents with billy clubs if the women did not "answer or do as expected." In 1970, when she was a teenager, members of what would become the Black Panthers were involved in two spectacular shootouts with the police at Desire. She describes a local housing authority management that failed to perform routine maintenance, and an incursion of drug-dealing gang members doing violent business in a community that had become a shadowy no-man's land.

And in fact, HANO's reputation was only getting worse. In

1994, HUD's Office of the Inspector General conducted an audit, visiting 150 units in a random sample. All 150 flunked HUD's basic quality standards. "Tenants live in indecent, unsafe, and unsanitary conditions," the resulting report charged. A subsequent GAO report cited a backlog of 21,000 oustanding work orders for routine maintenance, and noted "structural problems such as missing ceilings and holes in walls, loose and peeling paint, steady leaks from faucets, and roach infestations." HUD revised its relationship with HANO, assuming still more control. For the fiscal year 1994-1995, HANO was scored lower on HUD's assessment scale than any other major housing authority in the country.

And crime? In April 1993, a triple killing left three bullet-riddled bodies at the end of a strip of the complex referred to at the time as "Cocaine Alley." In 1994, when Desire was down to roughly 900 residents, there were 14 murders at the complex. By then, many of the units were in such physical disrepair that they were uninhabitable, and it seemed as if anyone who had another option was taking it: "People were tired of seeing people's head blown off, or children walking to school would happen to walk over a dead body," Davis says. "People had gotten to the point where a gunshot didn't even matter to them, because they heard it so regularly." A majority of Desire's units were vacant, even at a time when there were more than 2,000 names on the waiting list for public housing in New Orleans.

"Words can't express how much we suffer here at Desire," Davis herself told *The Times-Picayune* in 1994.

No wonder that in the summer of 1995, when the process of tearing down Desire officially began, it seemed like cause for celebration. Admittedly, the new Desire would have only half as many units as the old one, but it still seemed that there would be a new home for every family still living in the complex. The mayor attended a special ceremony to kick off the destruction, and so did then-HUD secretary Henry Cisneros, who smashed a few ceremonial bricks with a mallet. A brass band played and residents joined in a second-line parade. "What a day!" said HANO's then-executive director. "Can you feel it?"

• • •

The celebratory mood did not last. By early 1997, apart from the destruction of 252 units, not much had changed at Desire. Local and out-of-state congressmen raised objections to the Desire plan and offered alternatives. At one point, a national consulting firm was brought in to assess whether the site was a "viable" one for public housing at all. Eventually another 408 units were torn down in 1998, and the plan was revised again, lowering the number of units in the envisioned final development to around 500. Still, nothing new had been built — and the trend toward tearing down without building up was starting to make some public housing residents and their advocates suspicious.

In most metropolitan areas, housing projects are hidden away in the fringes. In New Orleans, many are woven throughout the city. One is just a couple of blocks from the tourist-beckoning French Quarter; I pass two complexes every time I drive to the gym. As Desire's revitalization sputtered, the fate of another development, one that sits on prime land, seized the city's attention: St. Thomas had nearly 1,385 units and some 2,000 residents before it was razed in 2000. Nearly all of the project's households reported incomes of less than 30 percent of the median family figure for the area (this would work out to about $8,200, using 2000 Census data). As happened with Desire the plan for how to redevelop the site evolved significantly, and has become an extremely controversial but apparently unstoppable scheme involving a Wal-Mart, a 100-unit condominium, 414 "market-rate" apartments, and exactly 70 units earmarked for families earning 30 percent or less than the city's median family income.

Pieces of other housing projects were also torn down. In 1994, HANO administered 13,521 low-income units. Today the agency says there are 8,645 public housing units in New Orleans. The demolition of Desire and St. Thomas alone accounts for the destruction of 3,149 units. As residents of Desire and some other New Orleans projects watched this unfold, they asked the obvious question: What happens to the majority of displaced residents who, as a matter of basic math, cannot move back?

Don Everard is the director of a nonprofit called Hope House that serves the St. Thomas area. To him there is no mystery about how the competing forces — getting on with the destruction and figuring out where residents would go — would ultimately be resolved. Tearing down buildings took top priority, he says, and displaced residents could fend for themselves. Decades of disrepair helped convert projects into menacing eyesores, beyond salvation, he argues. "The Housing Authority would probably say they didn't have the resources to respond to this," he says. "I would say that it was demolition by neglect."

Housing officials did not have much to say to me about it at all. HUD referred inquiries to HANO. HANO asked for a faxed set of questions. Some it ignored, the rest it responded to, tersely, in writing. Asked for a response to past criticisms of the agency from the Inspector General's office and others that it had frittered away too much time and money on administrative fees and the like without doing much in the way of actual revitalization, a spokesman for the agency wrote: "In the absence of new construction, this would appear to be the case, however, the new [administration's] focus on construction of new units should bring the comparison more into line."

Regarding other past criticism, the spokesman wrote that the agency prefers to look toward the future.

• • •

The earlier versions of the Desire revitalization had been envisioned in phases. Tenants would be moved from certain buildings. Those buildings would be torn down. HANO gave displaced residents options. They could move elsewhere in Desire or elsewhere in New Orleans public housing, and then as the old buildings were replaced, have a chance to move back. Or they could leave the public housing system. As new units were built, the process would repeat. Doris Barber had lived in one of the very first buildings to be torn down, and had moved to another part of Desire in 1992. In the summer of 2001 she was still waiting to see the new units that she thought she would be moving into. Then the plan changed: Now HANO said that all the Desire buildings would have to come down before any new units could be built, for reasons having to do with infrastructure improvements such as laying new sewer lines, cutting new streets, and so on.

By this point, only about 50 families were still living in Desire's last buildings. "HANO sent letters to families stating that they needed to move," according to the agency spokesman. The teardown process was causing power failures and creating a dangerous situation. "Please take action immediately to relocate to other suitable housing," the letter said. As had happened at each stage of Desire's depopulation, residents were advised in writing of their options — moving within the system, participating in another low-income housing program, or leaving altogether.

Davis began telling her fellow tenants that they did not have to leave, that they should not leave, that the time had come to stop believing in the promises of housing officials and hunker down. They had heard promises of a "new Desire" for more than a decade and had seen nothing but destruction. They had come to believe that the system just wanted them to go away. Davis said the only way she would leave is if someone showed up and arrested her.

"When I decided to stay here," Doris Barber says, "I had a lot of people telling me it was foolish. 'They're not gonna build, they're not gonna do anything.' I had people telling me it would be dangerous. As if it wasn't dangerous all those other years with the things we had going on!" she says with a laugh. And so in September of that year the Desire Area Residents Council filed a lawsuit alleging that the eviction notices had violated a written agreement HANO had with Desire tenants over decision-making procedures affecting the site's redevelopment.

"We take a beating," Davis says, as she talks about the suit and her frustration with so many years of promises from politicians and bureaucrats at every level of government. For the first and only time in our conversations, she is becoming emotional, and it happens gradually as she speaks; her tone of voice hardly changes, but the look in her eyes gets steadily harder. "In spite of the lawsuit we're still taking a beating.... Our people scattered all over. They're crying out for help. There's no help. There's no organization of agencies that can bring the necessary help....If this would have happened, an unexpected bomb were to visit a city, they would eventually have brought some kind of help. You know? We didn't have a physical explosion, but you definitely had some kind of demonic spiritual explosion."

Davis believes that what happened at St. Thomas could still happen at Desire — that this "prime land" could end up falling mostly into the hands of private developers, who reduce the public housing component as near to zero as possible, and let those who can't fight their way back in fend for themselves.

Later I spoke with Jim Hayes, a local housing expert who works with a nonprofit called the People's Institute for Survival and Beyond. He's been a tenant advocate for about 38 years. His view of Desire was a little different. While St. Thomas really did sit on prime land, Desire does not. It's inconvenient, surrounded by industry, and has a history of flooding. Thus he is "ambivalent" about the tenants' victory, basically suggesting that HUD and HANO are letting Desire tenants get away with it because the stakes are much lower than at the much-fought-over St. Thomas site. "They're going to get their housing," he says, "because they're out of sight, and out of mind."

Last summer, a judge issued a ruling in the Desire holdouts' favor. HANO has since renovated their units as the judge ordered. You can chalk this up to the rule of law, the grace of God, or the indifference of a system that has more important battles to fight. Either way, Davis and her neighbors had won the right to remain in the remnants of Desire.

• • •

According to HANO, there were 590 families in Desire in early 1995. Everyone would have the right to come back, HANO says, although each will "have to go through a screening criteria." That said, HANO acknowledges that only 397 of those families are still in its database. Of those, 244 currently live in other housing projects. (A number of former residents of St. Thomas and other demolished developments have gone to other projects as well, occasionally becoming an unwitting source of friction when they are placed in units that those projects' current residents coveted).

Another 153 former Desire residents are now part of what's called the Section 8 program: Displaced tenants can use a voucher-like certificate to rent from private landlords for roughly the same amount they had paid for public housing (plus utility bills, which are covered in public housing rents), with the government making up the difference. The big problem is both a shortage of vouchers and, more crucially, a shortage of landlords willing to take them — housing advocates report that 85 percent of New Orleans landlords refuse to participate in the Section 8 program. At last count the waiting list for Section 8 housing in New Orleans contained 16,000 names. Relocated families jump to the top of that list, and HANO says no such families are on it now.

Many Desire residents who went the Section 8 route have ended up in New Orleans East, even further from the city's core, in neighborhoods that are mostly poor. Bus ridership has declined in New Orleans, the head of the transit authority has explained, partly because bus routes are still patterned around the locations of now-disappeared housing projects, while New Orleans East — where the number of low-income residents is growing — remains under-served.

I drove out to New Orleans East to meet Sally Lee, a former Desire resident who is 88 years old. She took a Section 8 voucher three years ago, after more than half a century in the project. She lives on a residential block of small houses; there's no one around and some trash on the street, but her carpeted one-bedroom is tidy and seems comfortable, decorated with photos of the 11 children she raised in Desire.

She promptly announces that she wishes she had not left the projects. Why? Her first Section 8 house did not work out when the landlord sold it and the new one did not join the program; in the meantime Lee, after half a century in public housing, didn't really understand what she needed to do to keep her Section 8 eligibility, and soon lost it. Davis got involved and helped convince HANO to reinstate her.

At Desire, Davis had showed me one of the abandoned units. It was a blasted-out mess, with cabinets and paint left over from the 1970s, debris strewn about, water damage and holes everywhere you looked. It was exactly what the imagination calls up when thinking of "the projects." Because the occupied apartments in Desire's last buildings have been renovated, they are far more livable, clean, with fresh paint and no obvious major problems. Sally Lee's house seemed just as nice, but her story hinted at what it is that Davis, Barber, and the others say they are so anxious to cling to.

Davis has some negative memories of crime and relations with police, but she also recalls times when those relations improved — like a police bus taking Desire kids to the beach at Lake Pontchartrain, or the on-site police substation that helped bring a stabilizing influence for the last few

years of the 1990s. (This has of course been torn down.) What she and the others underscore is how outsiders fail to understand that despite the hardships of project life, it does foster communities — neighbors who look after each other's children, who share information, who are, in effect, each other's safety net. Squaring the idea of "community" with the hellish reality of, for example, blood-splattered bodies in the alleyways, is not easy. But this is the whole point of Lee's story, as she sees it: HANO did not help her, her old neighbor did.

• • •

A skeptic could easily say that this is nothing more than the "sentimental attachment" that so flabbergasted *The Times-Picayune*. Still, to Davis and the others, this bond sometimes seems all they have, after more than a decade of waiting for the government to make good on promises to revitalize Desire, and not simply obliterate it.

HANO's current plan promises 283 public-housing-eligible, townhouse-style rental units. Another 142 units will be made available to renters with a low-income housing tax credit. Also, 150 units have been added in the form of an "affordable homeownership" program. As units are completed, HANO says it will "administer another survey" of the former Desire residents it has kept track of, and this will determine who wants to come back — and who can come back. (As of

February 2003, HANO is no longer accepting new public housing applications.) Obviously, the 14 families that are still there are in the best position to get into the new units. And while they still worry that somehow, after everything, it might never come to be, they are also hopeful.

Today the spot that Doris Barber moved to in 1956 looks much as it must have when she and her husband took those long bus trips. "When I first looked at it again, it was kind of depressing," she says. "It was just demolition. But since all the lights have been put up, I can see everything from my bedroom window. I can stand in my bedroom window and look over the whole area.

"I can see Canal Street," she continues, her voice getting brighter and brighter as she talks. "I can see 'em building. All the streets are being put in. And it makes me feel good to see this. I'm happy now. We didn't waste our time staying here for nothing. And we're going to hang in here. Because with God all things are possible." She pauses and says earnestly: "You have to believe. "

MARCH 2003

golden arrow

3pm

I'm at the corner of Salcedo St. and Orleans Ave., just a couple of blocks from our house. The avenue is lined with people. A parade is passing. Here comes a group of men, black men, dressed in wildly elaborate Indian costumes, covered head to toe in feathers and beads, with headresses jutting up into the air. Out front is a guy in orange feathers, his face painted white with red stripes, waving a rifle (not a real one) whose barrel is covered by a feather-and-bead sheath that says "Spyboy." Behind him the Indians are in a cluster, dancing as they march to a tambourine rhythm that seems more Caribbean than Native American. At the center, in a huge, brilliant pink costume is Big Chief Peppy. He tosses out phrases as the others chant "oohm-ba-day," over and over.

I've been watching Big Chief Peppy all day. His "gang" (that's the preferred term) is called the Golden Arrows. It's one of many gangs in the parade today, a parade of Mardi Gras Indians, the reason that all these people are out in the street even though Mardi Gras was weeks ago.

Mardi Gras Indians are among the symbols of the city; in fact there's one on the cover of my *Time Out Guide To New Orleans*. Some people are kind of obsessed with them, not least because almost everything about them is mysterious. They appear on Fat Tuesday and have for decades, traveling through various black neighborhoods, and sometimes appearing in parades. They gather on Claiborne, the avenue that was once a leafy thoroughfare and is today a concrete stretch underneath an interstate. ◉ They come out also on other days, including this April Sunday, for special parades that are basically just showcases for the Indians. Some Indians perform at Jazz Fest. Fully outfitted, they are celebrities.

What's always interested me about the Indians is the nature of their celebrity. So much of life is a struggle between authenticity and persona — who we really are and who we pretend to be in various situations. The Indian persona is a particularly extreme and elaborate one, so much so that the

◉ SEE THE STORY "UNDER THE FREEWAY."

masked identity obliterates the one underneath. It seems nonsensical to make a celebrity of someone without having the slightest idea who he really is. I look at a given Big Chief and I often wonder: Who is that, underneath those feathers?

As the Golden Arrows move past, and another group of Indians appear, I turn to go home. This gang is singing "Shoo-Fly," which for some reason I've been hearing repeatedly today. On Salcedo, a young biker dude in a Lakers outfit, his motorcycle a matching yellow, is dancing for an audience of no one. Six or seven guys on horses trot by. A Jaguar pulls up beside me, and the man inside reaches his hand out the window to secure the mass of blue feathers that's strapped to the top of the car (part of someone's costume, I guess). He zooms off, and I pedal home.

Twenty minutes earlier

I arrive at the corner of Orleans and Salcedo, and the parade is hitting this corner just as I pull up. A big sign on wheels shows the painted image of an eye shedding tears, and says, "The universal tear of child is man's shame." I guess it has some religious implication.

Carnival is often considered from the high-society point of view — the white point of view.◉ Blacks (whether of African or Caribbean descent) were excluded from the season's official

◉ SEE THE STORY "HIGH SOCIETY."

celebrations for many decades, and developed a whole separate Mardi Gras culture, one that seemed to spring organically from the streets. For a time these traditions faded when Carnival became more integrated, but today, like everything else in New Orleans, they seem impervious to time itself.

The parade chugs by. First comes a Social Aid & Pleasure Club. "Benevolent Aid Societies" came about as an alternative to insurance for non-whites who could not obtain it: Members paid dues and created a pool they could use to cover health costs, or at least funeral costs. They would also join the second line at jazz funerals, and today several SAPCs are known as highly organized and talented paraders, with matching outfits and elaborate moves. I missed this group's name, but they wear matching shorts, suspenders, bow ties, and fedoras that they toss into the air. Then comes a brass band; people are singing "Shoo-fly." One of the little kids in the SAPC does a split in the street. After 10 minutes the first Indian appears. Then half a dozen, maybe 10 more. Then a man on stilts, costumed like something out of a Caribbean style Carnival parade. More "Shoo-fly," another man on stilts. Then came men in skeleton outfits — "bone gangs" being another black carnival tradition of mysterious origin (some theorize that it came from Haiti). One seems to have a pelvic bone strapped to his face. More Indians. One Indian gang is accompanied by skeleton men, with perfectly round skull masks, reminding me of The Residents. They're carrying gigantic bones. With them also are a lot of drummers.

This parade begins on Bayou St. John, several blocks away, and hundreds of people turn out to watch. That crowd on the bayou is probably half white, and includes at least some tourists. A few of these people join in the parade, and it's amusing to see them dancing along as the procession reaches this corner, which is not far away, but where the crowd is about 95 percent black. From here the parade goes on past the Lafitte housing project, and then, I believe, along Claiborne, under I-10.

I'm next to a parked van, and the guy sprawling in the driver's seat, with the door open, is yelling at one of the Indians. Finally he gets the Indian's attention, and the Indian, all in blue feathers, comes over, while the guy gets out of his van. They're both young, muscular guys in their 20s. They do that chest-bump semi-hug thing, and then the blue Indian says, "Check me out, nigga!"

Forty minutes earlier

On Bayou St. John there's a big expanse of grass, and a strip of it has been blocked off with police barricades, so the parade can form. It was supposed to start at 1:30, but hasn't yet. The SAPCs are lined up, and a few Indians, and there's a quick drum roll that makes me think it's about to start, but it isn't. Looking beyond the crowd, about a fifty yards from where I'm standing, I can see a shirtless guy who is dancing, apparently, on top of a van.

After five or so minutes, the music abruptly kicks into high gear and the parade starts moving. It takes a good half hour for the whole thing to move out, because it's only after the first wave starts going that various Indian gangs start wandering over. Big Chief Peppy and the The Golden Arrows queue up at around 2:20. As they move down the line, I go for my bike, but there are still at least 20 or 30 Indians milling around, gearing up to go.

Where did this tradition come from? As usual the answers are imprecise. One prominent theory is that it all started with a visit from Buffalo Bill's Wild West Show in 1884. Once I went to a talk at a local museum, during which various experts seemed pretty skeptical about that idea. They suggested there is evidence that blacks and Native Americans had made common cause before that event. Another thought is that the founder of the first parading gang, the Creole Wild West, had some Native American blood. One of the panelists that night was a semi-retired Big Chief, who talked about the period some decades ago when the gangs would, in the process of trying to out-do each other, resort to violent street fights. Maybe that's true. He was a strict traditionalist, and among other things said that "Shoo-Fly" is not a "real" Indian song. What struck me was the way this man talked — it was clear that to him there was simply nothing more exalted in life than to be a Big Chief. When he was not playing that particular role, he worked in a factory.

Thirty-five minutes earlier

Big Chief Peppy stands with his arms spread wide. He is surrounded by admirers. Almost everyone here seems to have a camera, a video recorder, or both. Old footage of Indians is rare, but there must be enough contemporary documentation to fill a museum. The circle around Peppy, shaking a pair of tambourines, tightens like paparazzi. His, orange-feathered spyboy (the lookout, when the Indians meander through neighborhoods) begins to bellow: "Big chief! Waaaay Uptown! Biiig Chief! Waaaaaaaay Uptown!"

They begin their chanting song, "Oohm-ba-day!" alternated with phrases tossed out by Peppy in a pleasantly commanding voice: "Sing it with me! (Oohm-ba-day!) Mm, Golden Arrows! (Oohm-ba-day!)" And so on. I suppose he's improvising. I try to note the phrases I can catch — "I've got religion / On my mind." "This little baby / Look so pretty." "I run through the river / I don't get wet / I walked through hell / Didn't break a sweat."

Some Indian gangs have essentially crossed over to become musical acts, performing in clubs and putting out CDs. The Wild Magnolias are probably the most famous example. The Golden Arrows appear on one CD, a 1998 compilation that included recordings by several gangs, called *United We Stand, Divided We Fall.*

More people crowd around and the spyboy dances in wild leaps, sometimes backwards. Some children scramble out of his way. He's huge in all those feathers, and there's no way he has the visibility in that costume to make sure he's not going to trample anybody as he moves. I don't know about the stories of the street fights back in the day, but there's no doubt that there's a threat of unspecified violence that hovers around the Indians — or if not that, then at least an assumption that everyone else will make way, and make way right now. And people tend to do that.

A man nearby is chatting up a young woman. "Nothing but soul," he's saying. "Ya heard me?"

After 20 or so minutes the crowd is getting too thick and I peel away. I'm wondering when the parade will start. I notice right then that one of the brass bands is just now arriving, leading a second line from the wrong direction on Orleans. In the other lane a city bus creeps along, trying to inch through the milling crowd.

Indian suits really are spectacular. When the insightful cultural critic Dave Hickey curated the 2000 International Bienniel for Site Santa Fe, he included a suit made by Big Chief Darryl Montana of the Yellow Pocahontas "Hunters."

Each Indian constructs a new suit every year, and they take a whole year to make, a hand-sewn assemblage of beads and feathers. Big Chief Peppy has already started on his 2004 suit.

One Hour and Thirty Minutes earlier

A Ford van marked Graebol Van Lines parks on the edge of Bayou St. John. Several men and women start unloading it.

One of the men is wearing a pink track suit. Only the shoes suggest that he's something other than a flashy eccentric. His name is Estabon Eugene. He's good-looking, trim, with a shaved head. It's hard to guess his age, but I suppose early middle age would be fair. Normally, he drives a cab. Today, he is preparing to transform himself into Big Chief Peppy. He fishes a few bucks out of his pocket for one of the children who will march with him. Later he helps the others get dressed — his spyboy, some others. He strolls over to chat to with another gang. Friends stop by to say hello. Just before the elaborate process of donning his own feathers begins, he munches on some Fritos. He looks like a regular guy.

APRIL 2003

zulu

I have here a photograph of a large man in blackface. He's holding a fake spear and a leopard-patterned shield and wearing a grass skirt. The photograph appears on the cover of the local alt-weekly's most recent Mardi Gras parade guide. The man is a member of Zulu, a Carnival krewe whose membership is predominantly black. On Fat Tuesday the Zulu parade rolls through the city's streets, through white neighborhoods and black neighborhoods and mixed neighborhoods, and everyone in the floats is dressed like this guy. It's an extremely popular parade.This year Spike Lee rode along as Zulu's guest of honor.

Friends and visitors ask from time to time about how race is viewed in New Orleans. I imagine leaving this picture of a grass-skirted man in blackface on the coffee table in our living room in New York, where we used to live, and how people would have reacted to it. If I leave it on the coffee table here, no one really notices. Is that good or bad?

The "old-line" krewes are at the center of Carnival's social season1.⦿ As some versions of the history have it, the Zulu parade actually came about partly as a satire of the absurd self-importance of those organizations: The first one, in 1909, had paraders wearing intentionally ragged clothes, and their "king" crowned with a lard can and hoisting a banana stalk as his scepter. The blackface, I gather, was part of the comedy. (Several elements of the early Zulu look were apparently borrowed from a contemporary musical comedy skit called "There Never Was A King Like Me.") Anyway, the parade grew and became a very big deal. In 1949, Louis Armstrong served as the monarch. "There's a thing I've dreamed of all my life," he told *Time Magazine*, "and I'll be damned if it don't look like it's about to come true — to be King of the Zulus' Parade. After that, I'll be ready to die."

Early on, the Zulu parade did not follow the same route as the big white krewes' parades. In fact it hardly followed a route at all, threading through the black neighborhoods of the segregated

⦿ SEE THE STORY "HIGH SOCIETY."

city, stopping at bars that had sponsored floats in exchange for a guarantee that Zulu would pay a visit. As an official Zulu history notes, "Once stopped at a sponsoring bar, it was often difficult to get the riders out of the establishment, so the other floats took off in different directions to fulfill their obligations."

Not surprisingly, some African-Americans were not impressed with the notion of blackfaced clowning. As *Time* put it back in 1949: "Among Negro intellectuals, the Zulus and all their doings are considered offensive vestiges of the minstrel-show, Sambo-type Negro." (Armstrong thought they were being uptight; he wore blackface in the parade.) In the 1960s, against the backdrop of the Civil Rights movement, the NAACP and other groups told Zulu they ought to knock it off, and at one point the group was down to 16 members.

• • •

In 1968 Zulu's route started to include St. Charles Avenue and Canal Street, where the tourists get to see it. While the rest of the route isn't random any more, it still goes through neighborhoods the main-line krewes ignore. Instead of reaching St. Charles via posh Napoleon Avenue, it comes from the corner of Claiborne and Jackson and gets to St. Charles by way of one of the truly blown-out ghettoes of New Orleans. Later, at Canal, where most of the parades essentially disperse near the French Quarter, Zulu continues along to Basin Street, and rolls past the

Iberville housing project. Then it heads up Orleans Avenue and jogs left on Galvez Street, going right through another project, the sprawling Lafitte.

This year was our fourth Mardi Gras, and we've always made it a point to catch Zulu. Usually we station ourselves on Jackson Street a block or two up from St. Charles, where the people density is a little less intense. I was pretty interested in getting a look at Spike Lee, because I wanted to know if he'd be wearing blackface. This year we ended up on the other side of St. Charles as Zulu rolled by, and we almost immediately spotted the float that Lee was on. He had no face paint, but wore a huge grin as he hurled beads and whatnot at the crowd. It struck me how rarely you see Spike Lee smiling.

• • •

The official Zulu history says nothing about satirizing Rex, and some accounts say those earliest parades weren't satires at all, they were just outrageous jokes, which is different. In any case, today The Zulu Social Aid & Pleasure Club is very much a part of official Carnival. Its king gets profiled in the newspaper, too. (The queen is not a young debutante, however, but simply the king's actual wife.) Zulu has a lot more than 16 members now. It has hundreds. Some are white. Recently I bought the Zulu 2003 Official Souvenir Book, which contains many, many pages of smiling, fez-wearing, black men. It also reveals that among

the white members is none other than Brobson Lutz (the man reduced to tears by the firing of a waiter at Galatoire's, elsewhere in this book). ◉

I read an interview with a guy who held one of the top Zulu offices last year — he was the Big Shot. (The Big Shot, one of the group's recurring "characters," smokes a huge cigar and tries to upstage the king.) A high school administrator, he said that he spent "in excess of $10,000" campaigning for the office. This year, somebody has taken out space on the billboard next to Zulu's headquarters on Broad Street to campaign for king. In

◉ SEE THE STORY "LUNCHEON."

other words, whatever its origins, Zulu today is a participant in the silliest aspects of Carnival, not a critique of them.

• • •

We had dinner a while ago with a visitor from D.C. who announced that "this seems like a very segregated city." I was basically dumbstruck, because I don't think of it that way, but of course we happened to be in a restaurant full of nothing but white people at the time. I might have said something to the effect that it's not immediately apparent to those visiting the northwest section of D.C. and eating in its trendier restaurants that the District as a whole is 60 percent black. But this is just another example of the easiest way to stalemate any discussion of race in America, which is to accuse the other side of hypocrisy. This tactic always works, for reasons that are obvious and sad. Anyway, how this visitor might have reacted to that magazine-cover photo of a blackface Zulu warrior I will never know — much to my relief.

Some time later on Fat Tuesday, we headed downtown again, racing ahead of the parade. Leaving our bikes locked up near a friend's house, we walked to a spot on the neutral ground across from the Iberville projects. Iberville is made up of low-rise brick buildings, and people crowded the second-floor balconies that face Basin. These must surely rank among the most coveted apartments in all of New Orleans public housing.

We yelled for beads and other throws (E got a frisbee), waited to get a second peek at Lee, and generally watched blackfaced float-riders tossing trinkets to a large, happy, and mostly black crowd. It might have been a good time for me to try and work out, once and for all, my answer to the question of how race is viewed in New Orleans. But of course, I didn't.

MAY 2003

st. james infirmary

This entry requires a short preamble. The story begins in
November 1998, before E and I had even moved to New Orleans.
And it is not over yet. The easiest thing to say is it is a story
about a song, "St. James Infirmary." Like most of the other
stories in this book, it was sent out by email to people who had
signed up for *The Letter From New Orleans*, and it was posted
on my web site. Unlike the other stories, it included a plea
for feedback and help; you could call it a mild attempt at "viral
reporting." Of course I wasn't sure how productive it would be,
since I was not researching a new trend or a nascent technology,
but a rather old bit of music. In practice, my experiment

did not travel the web as quickly as, say, a scatological Flash joke, but it did yield some interesting results. Even months after the fact, fellow "St. James" obsessives were stumbling upon the link and sending me their thoughts and suggestions, and even fresh facts, some of which have been worked in below (although 95% of what follows is the original June 2003 version of the story). Amusingly, one of the best tips I got turned out to be from someone who lived near my New Orleans neighborhood. There's the power of the Internet for you. In any case, when I say that the story is still not complete, I mean it: If you have something to add, I'm at walker@robwalker.net, and anxious to hear it.

— R.W.

• • •

So: November 1998. We were visiting the city with a bunch of friends, sharing a house in Gentilly for Thanksgiving. One night some of us went to Donna's, in the Quarter, where the Hot Eight was playing. They did a version of "St. James Infirmary." I had heard St. James Infirmary a number of times, and liked it quite a bit. But this was the first time I'd really thought about the curious lyrics.

The leader of the Hot Eight was a wild young trumpet player, alleged age 18, with glasses and big, baggy jeans. He seemed to blow with all his strength, with all his savvy, sometimes letting his left hand dangle and arching his body back and *forcing* out the notes. I got the impression that the Hot Eight might be an unruly bunch in general, one reason being that we saw them a couple of times and there were never eight of them — only six or seven showed up at a time.

Anyway, he sang the opening stanza in a rather subdued and mournful tone, which the other players matched. Those lyrics went like this:

> *I went down to St. James Infirmary,*
> *Saw my baby there.*
> *She was stretched out on a long white table, so sweet,*
> *so cold, so bare.*
>
> *Let her go, let her go, God bless her.*
> *Wherever she may be,*
> *She can search this whole wide world over,*
> *She ain't never gonna find another man like me.*

So I'd heard the lyrics before, but now I was thinking about them. Sad song about a man going to see the corpse of his lover....And will she go to heaven or will she go to hell...And whatever the answer, she "ain't never gonna find another man like me." Wow. That's something. That's beautiful and wrong at the same time.

The music continued, and the way the Hot Eight did it, they eventually came back around and repeated this opening verse. But now the funeral march pace was gone and it was a wailing dance, a celebration, an affirmation — body arched back, left hand dangling, forcing out those notes — SHE AIN'T NEVER GONNA FIND ANOTHER MAN LIKE ME.

• • •

So that stuck with me. After I moved here, and was in a position to hear a lot of the local standards in a variety of settings — outdoor festivals, small clubs, parades, jazz funerals — "St. James Infirmary" became my favorite. I got mildly curious about it one day. I knew there was a very famous Louis Armstrong recording, which I happened to have on some best-of CD reissue. The notes there said it was recorded on December 12, 1928, in Chicago, and listed the writer as J. Primrose. Armstrong did the lyrics pretty much as the Hot Eight were doing them 70 years later. Now I paid more attention to the next verse, which (in Armstrong's rendition) goes:

When I die, I want you to dress me in straight-laced shoes
Box-back coat and a Stetson hat
Put a twenty-dollar gold piece on my watch chain,
So the boys will know that I died standin' pat.

I liked that, too. It was odd that the singer would abruptly start addressing his own funeral arrangements while looking at his lover's body, but I found it charming somehow. I'm not saying I admire the narrator, who seems overly pleased with himself and dishonest besides. But I do admire something in his matter-of-fact, fearless taunting of the fates. That just seems very New Orleans to me.

• • •

I was pleased to discover that Sarah Vowell, whose work on "This American Life" I have enjoyed, had written about "St. James Infirmary," in an October 6, 1999, piece for Salon.com. I've since found that some of the specifics in that article are off, but she is certainly right in identifying the source of the song's curious pull in that jarring moment when the singer turns away from the horror of death and abruptly starts bragging about his own superiority to all men in this world or any other.

Vowell's take is that the shift "doesn't make any sense unless you take into account the selfish way the living regard the dead....[T]he narrator of this song is curiously so stuck up that he feels sorry for his loved one, not because she won't be doing any more breathing, but because she just lost the grace of his presence. It's so petty. And so human." Not only that, the song also "shoots down the idea of love as a true possibility. If you need love in part to know you'll be missed when you're gone, what does it mean if your sweetheart stands over your icy corpse and — instead of wishing to rejoin you on some astral plane — fantasizes about impressing his buddies with a big dumb coin?"

Well, okay, that's intriguing, but also a little harsh, and it's not how I see things. And I couldn't stop thinking about the song. What did it mean? Where did it come from? I began to concoct theories that would perhaps redeem the singer. My most clever interpretation, I think, was that perhaps the singer had killed his lover in a jealous rage. Perhaps she'd been cheating on him, and he caught her in the act. That would explain both his strange insistence on informing her corpse that he's the best man she'll ever have, and also his preoccupation with his own death, perhaps by execution.

Anyway, fast forward a few months and I own several dozen versions of "St. James Infirmary," which is a fair indication of the intensity that my interest in the song would eventually reach. I have renditions by Cab Calloway, Benny Goodman, the Hall Johnson Negro Choir, Red Garland, Harry Connick, Jr., The Animals, Bobby "Blue" Bland, The Ventures, The White Stripes, and Marc Ribot. As Vowell notes, the song is sometimes listed as traditional, but is more often attributed to Joe Primrose or to Irving Mills, "an associate of Duke Ellington."

Actually Joe Primrose is Irving Mills. I eventually confirmed this with EMI Music, the song's publisher. According to EMI, Mills, using the pseudonym Joe Primrose, took the copyright on the song in 1929. This seemed odd, if it's right that the Armstrong recording was actually made in late 1928. A knowledgeable reader has suggested that Mills probably published the song in 1928 and deposited the copyright the following year; publishers, my correspondent added, often sent artists advance copies of their tunes.

A lot has been written about (and by) Louis Armstrong, and I certainly have not read it all, but I have looked through many books for clues to how he might have come to record this particular number. I've found nothing solid. I was reading through a book called *Storyville, New Orleans*, by Al Rose, in particular a passage about the corner of Bienville and Marais streets. (This corner no longer exists; there's a housing project where Storyville used to be.) Jelly Roll Morton hung out at one of the bars on that corner, and across the street stood St. James Methodist Church. "According to a common legend," Rose writes, "the church offered first-aid services and modest hospital facilities and thus became the inspiration for the widely performed St. James Infirmary Blues."

Ah!

But no. The next line: "Unfortunately, this colorful and imaginative legend is not true; indeed, the song has no connection with New Orleans." After this crushing sentence,

Rose moves on to his next topic, without a footnote or a backward glance. But I now have a pretty good idea what he meant, because this particular story really begins, at the very latest, in 1790.

• • •

"St. James Infirmary," it turns out, is an offshoot of an extraordinary song cycle that is the subject of a 1960 Folkways Records release called *The Unfortunate Rake: A Study In The Evolution of A Ballad*, containing 20 songs and extensive notes by Kenneth S. Goldstein. I have, needless to say, purchased this item. Goldstein writes that the oldest published text from the "Rake" cycle was "collected" in 1848 in County Cork, Ireland, "from a singer who had learned it in Dublin in 1790." The song may have been "in tradition" for years prior to that, but it's obviously impossible to say. (He also notes that St. James Hospital was in London, and treated lepers.)

The disc includes one recording based on lyrics printed on a 19th century broadside. The singer recounts "a-walking down by St. James Hospital" one day and running into a friend, who was "wrapped up in flannel," despite the warm weather. The friend blames his troubled health on "a handsome young woman." It seems that he knew this woman rather well, but there was something she didn't tell him, and if only she had, "I might have got the pills and salts of white mercury." This refers to a treatment for venereal disease. "Now I'm cut down in the height of my prime," the unfortunate rake explains, proceeding to make requests relating to his funeral ("Get six of your soldiers to carry my coffin, six young girls to sing me a song…").

The next several tunes on the disc are variations on this story, with the lyrics rearranged in various ways. One difference is that most are explicit that the young man is a soldier or sailor, and none are anywhere near so explicit about what exactly his problem is. In fact they're all extremely vague — it's just a young man who is "cut down in his prime" for reasons that aren't clear. Sometimes, as in "Bad Girl's Lament," the ballad is about the woman, but basically follows the same pattern (an early mention of St. James' Hospital, a closing request for "Six pretty maidens with a bunch of red roses, six pretty maidens to sing me a song…"). You won't find many of these exact same words in the most typically played version of "St. James Infirmary" today, but this at least is a back story that makes some of the latter's sentiments perfectly logical: The singer makes a jealousy-tinged boast and turns quickly to thoughts of his own death because his "baby" just died of VD. Dig?

• • •

The ballad traveled the world. There is a black West Indian version from the 19th century. And there's one from Kentucky (dated to 1915) that seems to have been adapted to refer to a specific local scandal involving a former policeman caught up in a brothel-based slaying that led to his own execution. Another version of the ballad traveled west with pioneers as "The Cowboy's Lament." It's basically the same story again, but the linen-wrapped fellow is a cowboy found on a Laredo street. ("Get sixteen cowboys to carry my coffin; get sixteen pretty ladies to bear up my pall..."). Sometimes the request is for a bunch of gamblers to carry the coffin.

Alan Lomax appears on the Folkways disc — singing. He contributes a "Negro version" of the ballad that he and his father collected in 1934 from a prisoner in Sugar Land, Texas. It's called "St. James Hospital." Here it's worth noting that up to this point on the disc, none of the versions has the melody of the modern "St. James Infirmary." (It's also worth noting that Lomax is not much of a singer.) Instead they use the melody closer to the one we know today as "Streets of Laredo," which has been recorded by Johnny Cash, Marty Robbins, Willie Nelson, Buck Owens, Arlo Guthrie, and many others. The "Rake" cycle splits in two directions, one leading to Laredo, the other to the St. James Infirmary. In Goldstein's notes, Lomax is quoted saying this version "provides the link between the folk ballad and the pop tune" — between "The Unfortunate Rake" and "St. James Infirmary."

The actual recording of the prisoner (James "Ironhead"

Baker) singing "St. James Hospital" appears on a Rounder CD of material collected by Lomax and his father John A. Lomax called *Black Texicans.* This is an interesting set, exploring and documenting black variations on and contributions to the cowboy ballad form. (The Lomaxes seem to have been particularly interested in prisoners who'd had little contact with the outside world, and thus with popular recordings and recent musical trends and so forth, for decades.) Oddly, despite the title, the words "St. James hospital" appear in Lomax's rendition, but not in Baker's. The melody may not be quite the same as the "Rake" melody, but despite what Lomax implies, it's hardly identical to "St. James Infirmary," which of course had been recorded by Armstrong about five years before the "Ironhead" Baker's performance in Sugar Land.

• • •

This raised more questions, and trying to answer them has been an interesting, if ultimately frustrating, process. We live in a moment of very intense documentation. Every cultural event — hell, every *wedding* — is captured on video, in photographs, written up in web logs and emails. The historians of the future will have an embarrassment of riches to work with, no matter how trivial their inquiries may be. And I sometimes wonder if they'll have much left to inquire about, given how few secrets are left in our real-time culture. It's startling to look back less than 100 years in search of answers, only to confront the alien idea of the unknowable.

We know that Irving Mills was born in New York, the son of immigrants from Odessa, Russia. As young men, he and his brother Jack worked as "song pluggers" (promoters), and in about 1920 they set up their own music-publishing firm, Mills Music. At the time, such firms made money by selling sheet music. Live performances and even recordings were basically seen as a way of promoting such sales. Jazz was commercially popular; Mills Music also sold novelty rags and blues. They would buy songs from musician-writers for a flat fee, and own them outright. They once bought all rights to 21 Fats Waller songs for $500.

The forward-looking Irving did a pretty good job getting involved with new technologies like radio, and was apparently a pioneer in sending free recordings to publications to garner publicity. (Recording sales overtook sheet music in the mid 1930s.) He also started working as an agent, most famously for Duke Ellington, under an arrangement that allowed him to take partial writing credit on dozens of early Ellington tunes, many of which he probably did not contribute to at all. For this reason, Mills is generally recalled as a bit of a scoundrel; just about every time I've read some passing mention of him in liner notes or jazz books, it's dismissive at best. There's so much more to say about Mills, but seeing as how he had little to do with New Orleans, I'll get to the point.

The point is this. In 1927, the poet Carl Sandburg published a book called *American Songbag*, a collection of 280 songs (music and lyrics and very short explanatory introductions) from "all regions of America." About 100 of these he describes as "strictly folk songs," never before published. "Though meant to be sung, [the book] can be read as a glorious anthology of the songs that men have sung in the making of America." One of the songs is called "Those Gambler's Blues." Two sets of lyrics are given for the melody, one collected from someone at the University of Alabama, the other given by two sources, one in Los Angeles and one in Fort Worth. There's no mention of a composer, which rather strongly implies that this is one of the folk songs with no known author, which these days we would see credited to "Traditional." The lyrics contain much of what we hear as "St. James Infirmary" today; the melody (I confirmed with a friend who reads music) is basically the same.

Again it's worth noting how the world has changed. Can you imagine someone today getting away with taking credit for writing a song that had actually been published in a collection — one compiled by a famous poet — two years earlier? Anyway, I don't know where Irving Mills heard the tune. I don't know why he used the name Joe Primrose in claiming it, as he never seems to have used that pseudonym again. I can tell you that the Harlem Hot Chocolates recorded a version in New York in March 1930, with a singer identified as Sunny Smith. This was actually Duke Ellington's band, with Mills, under another pseudonym, on vocals. He's not a great singer, but he's better than Alan Lomax.

The only recording I've been able to find that pre-dates Armstrong's is a performance by Fess Williams and his Royal Flush Orchestra, made February 25, 1927 in New York City. On the CD version, the song is listed as "Gambler's Blues," and, maddeningly, the writer credit is "Moore-Baxter." Reader and fellow "St. James" obsessive Robert W. Harwood, in his cool self-published book *A Rake's Progress*, explains that drummer Carl "Squeakin' Deacon" Moore and bandleader Phil Baxter essentially gave a lightly comic spin to the traditional tune. Even more maddeningly, I also came across a single stray reference to Don Redman as the song's writer. Jorma Kaukonen (formerly of Jefferson Airplane and Hot Tuna) covered the song not long ago and credited it to Jimmie Rodgers, who cut a version under the title "Those Gambler's Blues" in 1930. I don't know what to make of these outliers. Maybe they are just mistakes.

The jazz reference books I've seen that address the question of the song's authorship tend to offer no specific name, but say that it dates back to 1910, or maybe the late 1890s, etc. In other words they don't help. Maybe the most definitive thing we can assert is that somebody who was at least partly inspired by "The Unfortunate Rake" laid down the blueprint for the song we now know as "St. James Infirmary" sometime prior to 1927, and that in 1929, "Joe Primrose" was granted the copyright.

• • •

Now, I'm generally skeptical of music writing that focuses on analyzing lyrics, and I deplore attempts to treat lyrics like poetry. However, I am obviously very interested in that one lyrical passage — the one in which the singer suddenly shifts from lamenting his lover's death to bragging that: "She can search this whole wide world over; she ain't never gonna find another man like me."

There's a lot of tweaking and futzing and rearranging of lyrics in various recorded versions of "St. James Infirmary" that I've heard. In the "Rake" songs the singer was a third-party narrator, relating a tale he heard from the stricken man himself. The oldest "Rake" songs downplay the woman, who is merely an undifferentiated "flash girl," not the unfortunate protagonist's true love.

This is even true of "Gambler's Blues." In the most prevalent version, the narrator is in a bar and hears the tale of woe from Big Joe McKennedy (or something similar), who is just back from having visited his lover's corpse at the St. James

Infirmary. (This is how Eric Burden did it, old school blues poseur that he is, in what I have to admit would be a great rendition if not for the backup singers going "oh-ooh-whoa" over and over.) But this scene of gazing at the woman's lifeless body is an addition to the storyline of the "Rake" songs, and suggests that the deceased was, in fact, the singer's true love, or at least main squeeze, not just an ill-advised fling.

Occasionally, the woman is immaterial or even eliminated. Dr. John reworked "St. James Infirmary" into "Touro Infirmary," a lament for the death of his hard-living "runnin' partner," who had requested "the finest whores on Bourbon Street" and Professor Longhair for his funeral, before he ended up dead on arrival at Touro (a real New Orleans hospital). One of the most extraordinary variations is Blind Willie McTell's "The Dyin' Crapshooter's Blues." McTell had done some recording — and like Mills was fond of pseudonyms, from Pig 'n' Whistle Red to Barrelhouse Sammy — but was reduced to singing in the street when an Atlanta recording shop owner came upon him in 1956 and made what turned out to be the last recordings of a gifted bluesman. At one point McTell sets up his next number by saying he started writing it in 1929 and finished it in 1932. It concerns a gambler friend named Jesse Williams, who was shot in the street, taken home by McTell, and as he died proceeded to give McTell a number of funeral-related requests — 16 crapshooter pallbearers, 16 bootlegers to sing him a song, and so on (plus a pair of dice in his shoes, a deck of cards as his tombstone, and a wish for "everybody to do the Charleston while he's dyin'"). The fact that Williams' woman had left him is a mere aside; the song has him killed by police for unspecified reasons. Williams, McTell relates, asked him to sing about all this at the funeral itself. "That I did," McTell asserts. "See, I had to steal music from every which a-way to get it, get it to fit." (Bob Dylan later wrote a song called "Blind Willie McTell," and an extensive deconstruction of that tune by Michael Gray in *Song & Dance Man III* is how I came to McTell and then to "Dyin' Crapshooter's Blues." Dylan's song, too, includes echoes from the "Rake," and ends, "I am gazing out the window of the St. James Hotel, and I know no one can sing the blues like Blind Willie McTell.")

Most of the more modern jazz versions (Armstrong forward) omit this narrative device and make it a first-person story. That passage I'm so obsessed with does not appear in the old English "Rake" songs, nor is it in either version of the lyrics provided by Sandburg, or in McTell's version. In one of the sets of lyrics that Sandburg offers, the line is replaced with, "There'll never be another like her; there'll never be another for me." This is the way the Hall Johnson Negro Choir did it in December 1931, and it's also the reading that Bobby Bland went with decades later. It's certainly a more traditional and less jarring sentiment. And it's much less interesting.

The line is omitted from Fess Williams' 1927 take, which skips straight from the image of the dead woman to the narrator discussing his own funeral. The version that Mills (as Sunny Smith) sang in 1930 basically has it both ways: After seeing his baby on that long white table, he first "wish[es] it was me instead," and then throws in the "search this whole world over" verse right afterward. Another version that Mills was involved with, recorded by Mills Merry Makers in January 1930, has Charlie Teagarden (younger brother of Jack) on vocals, and delivers a take that works so hard to get the verb tense right that it sounds like a grammar teacher delivered it: "She *could have looked* this wide world all over, *she'd never have found* a sweet man like me." (Emphasis added.) It's actually a nicely done vocal, but that reading of the line is ridiculous, and completely misses the mysticism and the nastiness of the eternal vengeance implied by saying that *even in the afterlife* she'll never find such a man. It also waters down the sense that the singer is affirming his own life with a certain proud desperation. Which to me is the whole point.

• • •

In New Orleans, the lyrics are pretty much always performed the way Armstrong did them. The most recent recorded version I know of is on 2002's *The Marsalis Family*, with patriarch Ellis and all four of his musician sons. Harry Connick sings — and uses the lyrics that Armstrong did.

How did the song come to Mills' attention? Did he hear a recording? A live performance somewhere? Where did Armstrong pick it up? Was it being played in New Orleans when he was growing up, hanging around Storyville? Who added that key lyrical phrase, "She'll never find another man like me"?

I don't know, I don't know. Maybe I never will. That Bob Dylan book I mentioned earlier led me, through its footnotes, to a 1975 book called *The Electric Muse: The Story of Folk into Rock*. One section, by a writer named Karl Dallas, deals with "St. James Infirmary" and "The Unfortunate Rake," and marvels at how "the soldier dying of syphilis in eighteenth century London crosses oceans, changes sex, becomes a cowboy dying of gunshot wounds on the streets of Laredo, coming to rest finally in New Orleans as the black hero of…'St. James Infirmary.'" Putting aside Dallas' unflinching association of the song with New Orleans, which obviously pleases me, I was interested in his point that the common bond is the dying protagonist in one way or another calling the shots of his own funeral. The requests, by and large, are not modest, despite the fact that in pretty much every case that protagonist admits that his pending death is the result of his own bad behavior (whether a single aberration or a lifetime of sin). "Though the identity of the hero and the cause of death changes, one thing remains — the triumphant laugh in the face of death." I actually think that overstates things for the earlier "Rake" versions, but it's right on target for "St. James Infirmary" as the Hot Eight performed it that night in 1998 — both in the specific words chosen, the way those words were sung, and the force of the music that accompanied them.

Since that key line in the Armstrong version does not have a precedent that I am aware of, I can at least pretend that this is the way he had heard it performed in New Orleans, before he left for Chicago in 1922. I have no proof of this at all, of course, but I think it is still too soon to say that the song has "no connection with New Orleans whatever." Because every time I hear some local brass band playing the tune, I always say to myself: "No connection with New Orleans? That just can't be right."

JUNE 2003

the toni morrison interchange

Driving on Carrolton Avenue from our neighborhood toward the river, you have to go through this highway snarl called the Toni Morrison Interchange. It's a drag. And there's this big sign that says, "Toni Morrison Interchange." I couldn't figure that out. Why would they name anything after Toni Morrison in New Orleans — and why, of all things, a highway interchange? Was there a ceremony? Did this winner of the Nobel Prize come down here and watch some official christen that dumb sign?

At the library one day I ran a cursory news-story search and found an article from the October 25, 1999, *Times-Picayune*. That's a few months before we moved to New Orleans. The headline: "Signs Honor Lawmaker, Not Writer." The interchange, it turns out, is named in honor of a different Toni Morrison — deLesseps S. "Toni" Morrison Jr. ("the son of longtime New Orleans Mayor deLesseps 'Chep' Morrison," the paper added). This Toni Morrison was a state representative in the 1970s and "led the fight to secure money to pay for the multilane I-10 bridge" that is now named in his honor. Morrison died in 1996, the interchange was named for him in 1997, and the signs went up, apparently, in 1999.

So that solves that, I guess. But I still like the idea that maybe, somehow, the interchange could also be a tribute to Toni Morrison, the author. I have long wanted to start an informal program to be called "The Toni Morrison Interchange," wherein Toni Morrison books would be left in modest quantities on the highly unpleasant pedestrian path that leads through this concrete knot. I'd like to do this because I often see people walking along it, and they never look happy. Maybe if there was a nice Toni Morrison novel there for them to pick up, it would make their day. Ideally, they would return the book to the same spot upon completion, so others might enjoy it — thus, an interchange. Perhaps this will happen some day. Perhaps not.

AUGUST 2003

a memorable encounter
at a grocery store

One day I'm standing in line at Sav-A-Center. It's not really a line, there are only two guys in front of me, and they're basically done. But they're engaged in some sort of conversation with the cashier, and it's lasting a while. I stand patiently, looking at tabloid headlines, waiting. Eventually she starts ringing up my stuff, but continues chatting with the two guys. I'm not really catching what they're talking about, but as it seems to be winding down, the cashier says, "Over by Rhodes." This is the name of a funeral home. The guys are nodding — yeah, they know where Rhodes is — and they're starting to walk away.

The cashier says, "I still do some embalming for them."

Right as she's saying this, she's putting my tomato on the scale.

She looks up at me. The two guys have left. Matter-of-factly, seamlessly, as if she had been talking to me the whole time, she says to me, "It's hard work, but it pays good."

I gather she means embalming.

She puts my onion on the scale.

I say: "Is that right?" I don't know what else to offer.

She continues, again as if we'd been having a conversation for the last 20 minutes, and explains how she used to embalm full-time, but doesn't anymore. Apparently she has friends in the business and picks up a little freelance work now and then. The going rate is $75 a body, $100 if the body is post-autopsy. She has worked at funeral homes where 8 or 9 bodies a day come in, although I get the impression that a lone person would not embalm all of them.

She's bagging my groceries now.

Because she has briefly stopped talking, the suggestion that we have been having a genuine conversation is so strong that I feel I must make a comment, or ask a question. So I say: "How did you get started doing that?"

Cheerily, she explains how when she was young, a lot of her relatives died, and she went to a lot of funerals, and got interested.

Then she says: "Credit or debit?"

Then she says that later, in school, she did a report on funeral homes, and one thing led to another. She says she considered opening her own funeral parlor but did not really have the business background for it. Finally she adds that it's just as well, she doesn't think she really would have wanted to do that, anyway.

I've got all my bags in hand at this point, and I'm just standing there, listening. She says, "It's real interesting work, though."

I say: "Yeah, sounds like it." And then I leave.

AUGUST 2003

the schloegel findings

Early in 2000, four of us were sitting around the living room: My mother, my father, E, and me. It was my parents' first visit since we'd moved to New Orleans. We were chatting. Then my mother said something surprising.

"Have you gone and looked for anybody in the cemeteries yet?"

I said, Well, we've been to some of the old cemeteries, but what do you mean, who would I be looking for?

"Schloegels," she said.

My great grandmother's last name was Schloegel (pro-nounced SHLAY-gull). She died when I was very young, but I have some faint memories of her. And anyway I still didn't understand my mother's point. So she explained: Before Grandma Schloegel and her husband and daughters moved to the midwest, the family had been in New Orleans for generations.

This was news to me.

My mother's maiden name, I knew, is Deupree. It turns out the Deuprees were among the French immigrants who were run out of Canada and ended up in and around New Orleans. My great grandfather was on the (German) Schloegel side, and he worked for a time sweeping floors at one of the city's newspapers. His father was a waiter at Antoine's, apparently for decades; when he retired there was, supposedly, a huge party for him that was written up in the paper.

Again, hearing all this was a surprise.

• • •

Even so, I can't say that I immediately became obsessed with this new information, and I'd better tell you right now that this story does not end with me tracking down distant relatives and finding we have surprisingly a lot, or surprisingly little, in common. In the three years that followed the Schloegel surprise, I asked a few questions, but useful answers were rare. My mother said she did not know the name of her great grandfather, the Antoine's waiter. My grandmother or her sister may have known something, but they are both dead. There are no old diaries or letters to consult. Any ties with distant relatives fell away long ago. As for checking cemeteries, how would I even know where to look? My older sister says she remembers, as a child, visiting a cemetery here with Grandma Schloegel, but nothing specific about it at all.

Then one day I typed some words into Google — probably "Schloegel" and "New Orleans" and "cemetery" — and, bizarrely, it resulted in something useful. Somebody had put online a listing of all the names on the tombs and headstones at Lafayette Cemetery No. 1. And one of the names was Schloegel.

Lafayette Cemetery No. 1, which is right across from Commander's Palace, is probably our favorite cemetery here. We'd been several times. Obviously I had never noticed a Schloegel. But now I had a map from that web site. So we went back, and there it was: A tomb about seven feet tall with a whole lot of names on it, the very first name being J. Anton Schloegel, 1814-1871. There were another 15 names on the tomb, but Schloegel was only part of two of them. There was M. Regina Schloegel, presumably Anton's daughter, who was born in 1870, and died two years later. Further down was

Rosalie Schloegel Pastoric, 1869-1936 — likely another daughter of Anton's.

• • •

Eventually I went to the library to see what I could accomplish by way of looking up marriage announcements and obituaries and other such things. I went through the little index cards in a row of big metal filing cabinets, and found a mess of Schloegels — almost 30 of them.

I figured out that J. Anton's wife, Barbara, remarried, to a man named Koch, and it was their descendents who mostly filled that Lafayette Cemetery tomb. Also I found an Andrew Schloegel, who died in 1895, at age 65, and was "a native of Neuberg an der Kammel del Brunlauch, Germany." I won't go into the numbing details, but I concluded that most of the other Schloegels I looked into were in one way or another related to or descended from this man. But what was his relation to J. Anton? They were 16 years apart, probably too close to be father-son, but also quite a gap for brothers.

Meanwhile, I was starting to feel pretty stupid for spending all this time drawing flow charts connecting Schloegels. I was becoming a Schloegelologist, but what was the point? There was still no clear link to me.

I called Antoine's. I thought maybe they would have a scrapbook or something. I told them that my great great grandfather had been a waiter there, and his last name was Schloegel. They were very patient with me. I believe they made efforts to see if they could come up with anything about this, but they couldn't. After all, I had so little information.

• • •

Recently I went to visit my parents at their house in Texas, and brought along what I'd started calling The Schloegel Findings. I liked the sound of that — like an old Woody Allen short story. I drove the long trip in a rental car, listening at times to one of those "lectures on tape" series — six hours on "The Self Under Siege." The lecturer talked about the gradual obliteration of the idea of the self by the forces of modernity, starting with the ideas of Nietshze, Freud, and Marx, and climaxing with the "fatal strategies" of Jean Baudrillard. The professor happened to be from West Texas. So it was with an extraordinary drawl that he described, for instance, Heidegger's ideas about the relationship between the anxiety brought on by the fear of nothingness and what it means for an individual to be a human being in the world.

If there is a worse thing to listen to before spending a few days with your parents in a part of the world that embodies what you've tried all your life to get away from, I can't think of it.

Anyway, I dragged out the Findings. I summarized what I knew, and I read off a bunch of the names that I hadn't had a chance to look into.

Apparently her grandfather, the son of the Antoine's waiter, was one of 11 children. It's plausible that in a brood of 11, there might well be a span of 16 years between two brothers. So maybe J. Anton and Andrew were siblings after all. There was certainly a great deal of overlap in certain names — there were a number of Antons and Anthonys among the descendents of Andrew. And if you exercise a certain ridiculous logic then you could even say: Well, if those two are brothers 16 years apart, maybe that somehow suggests that they are part of that crowd of 11 boys and thus my ancestors!

Back in New Orleans I looked in the phone book. There was an August Schloegel, a Hermann Schloegel, and a Regina Schloegel.

• • •

A while ago I read a long article that sort of meditated on Florida as an idea. Part of the writer's thesis was that Florida is a place that people "come to erase the past and make themselves new again." I guess it's true that Florida is a place where people go to reinvent themselves. They also go to New York City. And Los Angeles. California in general, really —

actually, the whole West. Certainly Texas. The Southwest. Alaska, too. Depending on where you're coming from you might also reinvent yourself in Chicago, or the South. If you're from anywhere else in the world, pretty much any place in America will do. Because, if you think about it, this supposed epiphany about the nature of Florida is in fact a lazy banality about the nature of America itself, dating back to the colonial period if not before: The ability to erase the past and make oneself new again is pretty much the whole point.

I did not ring up any of the New Orleans Schloegels and start asking to see their scrapbooks or whatever. Over the years, from time to time, people have asked me casually about certain family history questions and I have answered, honestly, that there are things I don't know. More than a few people have suggested that I have a "right" to know more.

One of the themes of the *Letter From New Orleans*, I belatedly realize, has been the idea of persona. I really do believe that the donning of a fresh and somehow idealized persona is a very American thing, and in a sense, the "masking" that pops up over and over here in New Orleans is just a particularly literal form of it. What's most interesting is that the "mask" is often an excuse to be uninhibited — to holler like an Indian chief or to waltz in the street, to do whatever else you may be too frightened or embarrassed to do in your day-to-day life. So which "you" is the true self, and which one is the constructed persona? If I had to settle on the one surprising line of thought that writing about New Orleans has led me to, this would be it. And to me, at least, it has meant a lot.

I realize that we live in a moment when people like to wallow in their confessed past, in best-selling books, on afternoon talk shows, anywhere they can find an audience.But the truth is that if America is about anything, it's about being able to forget the past if you want to.

AUGUST 2003

postscript

I always referred to the *Letters* as "pointless," but of course
that's not strictly true. I started writing them as a way to share
little stories with friends, and then with strangers, but I was also
interested in seeing what sort of an audience might emerge. I
write for a living, but there's not much of a market for stories
like these, so I was also interested if seeing whether, in some
indirect way, one might be created. What happened in the
meantime was that the informal market for online writing came
to be dominated by the blog phenomenon. Blogs are great, but
the most widely read ones stress brevity and timeliness — just
like the commercial market for nonfiction. Oh well.

Failure to reshape literary landscapes notwithstanding, I could not be more pleased with the audience that did develop for the *Letters*. It was not unusual for me to get more thoughtful and passionate feedback about a *Letter* than about articles I've done for publications with millions of readers. On this level it was a fascinating and rewarding experiment. But I believe that I have taken it as far as I can go.

In any event: Thank you for reading.

CREDITS AND ACKNOWLEDGEMENTS

A number of the photographs on the preceding pages are (or were) part of a planned project called "MLK Blvd." This was an idea that came about some years ago and has since languished. Many cities have a street named for Martin Luther King Jr., and MLK Blvds everywhere seem to have an awful lot of abandoned property, scary-looking bars, and small groceries that accept food stamps. At first I thought it would be interesting to do some sort of book, a photo book, on the subject of this "legacy." My latest thought is to create a web site, and turn "MLK Blvd" into an "open source" journalism project — interested parties could send in their own photos, or histories, or interviews, or documents, which I could then organize on the site. It could be open-ended. It would be a great thing for students of journalism or sociology or urban planning to participate in.

I realize that this is still vague. Maybe someday. Since I first thought about this, I have learned that a short film has been made about MLK Blvds for the Discovery Times channel, and also that a book called *Along Martin Luther King: Travels on Black America's Main Street* by Michael Falco, was published in November 2003. I still like the web site idea. We'll see. If you have thoughts about "MLK Blvd," or would like to offer help or suggestions, or you simply want to be informed if anything ever comes of it, write to walker@robwalker.net.

• • •

"To New Orleans" first appeared in the "Diary" section of *Slate*. The first day's entry was reprinted in the book, *The Slate Diaries* (Perseus, 2000). "Carnival" first appeared as Letter From New Orleans #1, the first installment in the (now concluded) series distributed via www.robwalker.net. "Three Percent Theory" was posted on robwalker.net before the Letter From New Orleans had come into being. "The Singing, The Song," which was Letter From New Orleans #2, was subsequently reprinted in the online magazine *KillingTheBudda.com*. "Death and After" was Letter #3. "Holiday Burning" was Letter #4. "Ernie K-Doe" was Letter #5. "Masked" appeared in *The New Republic*. "Yvonne's," which was Letter #6, was reprinted in the magazine *Perla*. "Ms. Flowers" first appeared as Letter From

New Orleans #7. "Under the Freeway" was Letter #8, and was later reprinted in the online magazine *Flaneur.com*. "Luncheon" was Letter #9. "Bohemians and Galatoire's: A Proposal" was written as a radio commentary for WWNO (New Orleans). "High Society" was Letter #10. "Golden Arrow" was Letter #11. "Zulu" was Letter #12. "St. James Infirmary" was Letter #13. "The Desire Line" was commissioned and paid for by *Mother Jones*, but was never published. "The Schloegel Findings" was Letter #14.

• • •

Thanks to the editors at the various publications mentioned above. Thanks to Fred Kasten of WWNO. Thanks to Myshkin (*myshkinsrubywarblers.com*) for letting me post the song "Yvonne's Bar" on the web site. Thanks to The New Orleans Historic Landmarks Commission for the photo of Yvonne's from 1995. Thanks to Daniel Samuels, author of "Remembering North Claiborne: Community and Place in Downtown New Orleans," and also to The Williams Research Center of the Historic New Orleans Collection, for help with "Under The Freeway." The book *Lords of Misrule*, by James Gill, was a great help to the writing of "High Society." Thanks to the following individuals for help, feedback, interest, or in several cases the simple willingness to put up with obscure questions from a total stranger on the subject of "St. James Infirmary": Cynthia Joyce, Raymond B. Landry, Alan Sirvent, David Fulmer, Jason Miller, Jim Lowell, Richard Heend, Jeff Parke, Calvert Morgan, Chris Tyle, John Hornsby, Morris Hodara (and here I'd like to plug The Duke Ellington Society, Box 31, Church Street Station, New York City 10008), David Hajdu, John Hasse, Tom Morgan, Gene Anderson, Bruce Raeburn, and in particular Robert W. Harwood

Thanks to Joley Wood for fine and helpful editing work. Thanks to G.K. Darby, whose decision to publish this book raises fresh questions about the line between courage and foolhardiness.

Thanks to my parents, for support, understanding, and love.

Thanks to E, for invaluable advice, for the site, for miscellaneous encouragement, and for everything else.